PAUL LAURENCE DUNBAR (1872-1906) was the son of former slaves. His father had fled to Canada before the Civil War; his mother was freed as a result of that conflict.

Dunbar published two collections of verse before *Lyrics of Lowly Life*, but it wasn't until the publication of this book in 1896 that he gained national recognition. The success of the book was no doubt spurred by its endorsement by William Dean Howells, one of the most respected literary figures of the day.

His later collected verse include *Lyrics of the Hearthside* (1899) and *Lyrics of Love and Laughter* (1903). Like *Lyrics of Lowly Life*, these volumes reveal the poet's bitterness about the oppression of his people.

Dunbar also wrote novels, the most popular of which was *The Sport of the Gods* (1902).

Jay Martin has edited an excellent collection of studies of the poet, *A Singer in the Dawn: Reinterpretations of Paul Laurence Dunbar* (Dodd, Mead & Co., 1974). There have also been biographies by Benjamin Brawley (1936) and Addison Gayle (1971).

Paul Laurence Dunbar.

Lyrics of Lowly Life

by Paul Laurence Dunbar

Introduction by
WILLIAM DEAN HOWELLS

A Citadel Press Book
Published by Carol Publishing Group

TO

MY MOTHER.

CONTENTS

———

vii

Contents

Contents

Contents

Contents

INTRODUCTION.

I THINK I should scarcely trouble the reader with a special appeal in behalf of this book, if it had not specially appealed to me for reasons apart from the author's race, origin, and condition. The world is too old now, and I find myself too much of its mood, to care for the work of a poet because he is black, because his father and mother were slaves, because he was, before and after he began to write poems, an elevator-boy. These facts would certainly attract me to him as a man, if I knew him to have a literary ambition, but when it came to his literary art, I must judge it irrespective of these facts, and enjoy or endure it for what it was in itself.

It seems to me that this was my experience with the poetry of Paul Laurence Dunbar when I

Introduction.

found it in another form, and in justice to him I cannot wish that it should be otherwise with his readers here. Still, it will legitimately interest those who like to know the causes, or, if these may not be known, the sources, of things, to learn that the father and mother of the first poet of his race in our language were negroes without admixture of white blood. The father escaped from slavery in Kentucky to freedom in Canada, while there was still no hope of freedom otherwise; but the mother was freed by the events of the civil war, and came North to Ohio, where their son was born at Dayton, and grew up with such chances and mischances for mental training as everywhere befall the children of the poor. He has told me that his father picked up the trade of a plasterer, and when he had taught himself to read, loved chiefly to read history. The boy's mother shared his passion for literature, with a special love of poetry, and after the father died she struggled on in more than the poverty she had shared with him. She could value the

Introduction.

faculty which her son showed first in prose sketches and attempts at fiction, and she was proud of the praise and kindness they won him among the people of the town, where he has never been without the warmest and kindest friends.

In fact, from every part of Ohio and from several cities of the adjoining States, there came letters in cordial appreciation of the critical recognition which it was my pleasure no less than my duty to offer Paul Dunbar's work in another place. It seemed to me a happy omen for him that so many people who had known him, or known of him, were glad of a stranger's good word ; and it was gratifying to see that at home he was esteemed for the things he had done rather than because as the son of negro slaves he had done them. If a prophet is often without honor in his own country, it surely is nothing against him when he has it. In this case it deprived me of the glory of a discoverer ; but that is sometimes a barren joy, and I am always willing to forego it.

Introduction.

What struck me in reading Mr. Dunbar's
poetry was what had already struck his friends
in Ohio and Indiana, in Kentucky and Illinois.
They had felt, as I felt, that however gifted his
race had proven itself in music, in oratory, in
several of the other arts, here was the first in-
stance of an American negro who had evinced
innate distinction in literature. In my criticism
of his book I had alleged Dumas in France,
and I had forgetfully failed to allege the far
greater Pushkin in Russia ; but these were both
mulattoes, who might have been supposed to
derive their qualities from white blood vastly
more artistic than ours, and who were the
creatures of an environment more favorable to
their literary development. So far as I could
remember, Paul Dunbar was the only man of
pure African blood and of American civilization to feel the negro life æsthetically and
express it lyrically. It seemed to me that this
had come to its most modern consciousness
in him, and that his brilliant and unique
achievement was to have studied the American

Introduction.

negro objectively, and to have represented him as he found him to be, with humor, with sympathy, and yet with what the reader must instinctively feel to be entire truthfulness. I said that a race which had come to this effect in any member of it, had attained civilization in him, and I permitted myself the imaginative prophecy that the hostilities and the prejudices which had so long constrained his race were destined to vanish in the arts; that these were to be the final proof that God had made of one blood all nations of men. I thought his merits positive and not comparative; and I held that if his black poems had been written by a white man, I should not have found them less admirable. I accepted them as an evidence of the essential unity of the human race, which does not think or feel black in one and white in another, but humanly in all.

Yet it appeared to me then, and it appears to me now, that there is a precious difference of temperament between the races which it would be a great pity ever to lose, and that

Introduction.

this is best preserved and most charmingly
suggested by Mr. Dunbar in those pieces of
his where he studies the moods and traits of his
race in its own accent of our English. We call
such pieces dialect pieces for want of some closer
phrase, but they are really not dialect so much
as delightful personal attempts and failures for
the written and spoken language. In nothing
is his essentially refined and delicate art so well
shown as in these pieces, which, as I ventured
to say, describe the range between appetite and
emotion, with certain lifts far beyond and
above it, which is the range of the race. He
reveals in these a finely ironical perception of
the negro's limitations, with a tenderness for
them which I think so very rare as to be
almost quite new. I should say, perhaps, that
it was this humorous quality which Mr. Dunbar
had added to our literature, and it would be
this which would most distinguish him, now
and hereafter. It is something that one feels
in nearly all the dialect pieces; and I hope
that in the present collection he has kept all

Introduction.

of these in his earlier volume, and added others to them. But the contents of this book are wholly of his own choosing, and I do not know how much or little he may have preferred the poems in literary English. Some of these I thought very good, and even more than very good, but not distinctively his contribution to the body of American poetry. What I mean is that several people might have written them ; but I do not know any one else at present who could quite have written the dialect pieces. These are divinations and reports of what passes in the hearts and minds of a lowly people whose poetry had hitherto been inarticulately expressed in music, but now finds, for the first time in our tongue, literary interpretation of a very artistic completeness.

I say the event is interesting, but how important it shall be can be determined only by Mr. Dunbar's future performance. I cannot undertake to prophesy concerning this ; but if he should do nothing more than he has done, I should feel that he had made the strongest

Introduction.

claim for the negro in English literature that the negro has yet made. He has at least produced something that, however we may critically disagree about it, we cannot well refuse to enjoy; in more than one piece he has produced a work of art.

W. D. HOWELLS.

Lyrics of Lowly Life.

ERE SLEEP COMES DOWN TO SOOTHE THE WEARY EYES.

E RE sleep comes down to soothe the weary
     eyes,
    Which all the day with ceaseless care have
       sought
The magic gold which from the seeker flies;
    Ere dreams put on the gown and cap of
       thought,
And make the waking world a world of lies, —
    Of lies most palpable, uncouth, forlorn,
That say life's full of aches and tears and sighs, —
    Oh, how with more than dreams the soul is
       torn,
Ere sleep comes down to soothe the weary eyes.

1

Lyrics of Lowly Life.

Ere sleep comes down to soothe the weary eyes,
  How all the griefs and heartaches we have
    known
Come up like pois'nous vapors that arise
  From some base witch's caldron, when the
    crone,
To work some potent spell, her magic plies.
  The past which held its share of bitter pain,
Whose ghost we prayed that Time might
    exorcise,
  Comes up, is lived and suffered o'er again,
Ere sleep comes down to soothe the weary eyes.

Ere sleep comes down to soothe the weary eyes,
  What phantoms fill the dimly lighted room ;
What ghostly shades in awe-creating guise
  Are bodied forth within the teeming gloom.
What echoes faint of sad and soul-sick cries,
  And pangs of vague inexplicable pain
That pay the spirit's ceaseless enterprise,
  Come thronging through the chambers of the
    brain,
Ere sleep comes down to soothe the weary eyes.

2

Lyrics of Lowly Life.

Ere sleep comes down to soothe the weary eyes,
  Where ranges forth the spirit far and free?
Through what strange realms and unfamiliar
    skies
  Tends her far course to lands of mystery?
To lands unspeakable — beyond surmise,
  Where shapes unknowable to being spring,
Till, faint of wing, the Fancy fails and dies
  Much wearied with the spirit's journeying,
Ere sleep comes down to soothe the weary eyes.

Ere sleep comes down to soothe the weary eyes,
  How questioneth the soul that other soul, —
The inner sense which neither cheats nor lies,
  But self exposes unto self, a scroll
Full writ with all life's acts unwise or wise,
  In characters indelible and known ;
So, trembling with the shock of sad surprise,
  The soul doth view its awful self alone,
Ere sleep comes down to soothe the weary eyes.

When sleep comes down to seal the weary eyes,
  The last dear sleep whose soft embrace is balm,

Lyrics of Lowly Life.

And whom sad sorrow teaches us to prize
   For kissing all our passions into calm,
Ah, then, no more we heed the sad world's cries,
   Or seek to probe th' eternal mystery,
Or fret our souls at long-withheld replies,
   At glooms through which our visions cannot see,
When sleep comes down to seal the weary eyes.

THE POET AND HIS SONG.

A SONG is but a little thing,
   And yet what joy it is to sing !
In hours of toil it gives me zest,
And when at eve I long for rest ;
When cows come home along the bars,
   And in the fold I hear the bell,
As Night, the shepherd, herds his stars,
   I sing my song, and all is well.

There are no ears to hear my lays,
No lips to lift a word of praise ;
But still, with faith unfaltering,
I live and laugh and love and sing.

4

Lyrics of Lowly Life.

What matters yon unheeding throng?
 They cannot feel my spirit's spell,
Since life is sweet and love is long,
 I sing my song, and all is well.

My days are never days of ease;
I till my ground and prune my trees.
When ripened gold is all the plain,
I put my sickle to the grain.
I labor hard, and toil and sweat,
 While others dream within the dell;
But even while my brow is wet,
 I sing my song, and all is well.

Sometimes the sun, unkindly hot,
My garden makes a desert spot;
Sometimes a blight upon the tree
Takes all my fruit away from me;
And then with throes of bitter pain
 Rebellious passions rise and swell;
But — life is more than fruit or grain,
 And so I sing, and all is well.

Lyrics of Lowly Life.

RETORT.

[handwritten annotation: head + heart: why are these separate? Look.]

"THOU art a fool," said my head to my
    heart,
" Indeed, the greatest of fools thou art,
  To be led astray by the trick of a tress,
By a smiling face or a ribbon smart ; "
  And my heart was in sore distress.

Then Phyllis came by, and her face was fair,
The light gleamed soft on her raven hair ;
  And her lips were blooming a rosy red.
Then my heart spoke out with a right bold air :
  " Thou art worse than a fool, O head ! "

ACCOUNTABILITY.

FOLKS ain't got no right to censuah othah
    folks about dey habits ;
Him dat giv' de squir'ls de bushtails made de
    bobtails fu' de rabbits.

Lyrics of Lowly Life.

Him dat built de gread big mountains hollered
    out de little valleys,
Him dat made de streets an' driveways was n't
    shamed to make de alleys.

We is all constructed diff'ent, d'ain't no two of
    us de same ;
We cain't he'p ouah likes an' dislikes, ef we 'se
    bad we ain't to blame.
Ef we 'se good, we need n't show off, case you
    bet it ain't ouah doin'
We gits into su'ttain channels dat we jes' cain't
    he'p pu'suin'.

But we all fits into places dat no othah ones
    could fill,
An' we does the things we has to, big er little,
    good er ill.
John cain't tek de place o' Henry, Su an' Sally
    ain't alike ;
Bass ain't nuthin' like a suckah, chub ain't
    nuthin' like a pike.

Lyrics of Lowly Life.

When you come to think about it, how it's all
    planned out it's splendid.
Nuthin's done er evah happens, 'dout hit's
    somefin' dat's intended;
Don't keer whut you does, you has to, an' hit
    sholy beats de dickens, —
Viney, go put on de kittle, I got one o' mastah's
    chickens.

FREDERICK DOUGLASS.

A HUSH is over all the teeming lists,
    And there is pause, a breath-space in
        the strife;
A spirit brave has passed beyond the mists
    And vapors that obscure the sun of life.
And Ethiopia, with bosom torn,
Laments the passing of her noblest born.

She weeps for him a mother's burning tears —
    She loved him with a mother's deepest love.
He was her champion thro' direful years,
    And held her weal all other ends above.

8

Lyrics of Lowly Life.

When Bondage held her bleeding in the dust,
He raised her up and whispered, "Hope and
      Trust."

For her his voice, a fearless clarion, rung
    That broke in warning on the ears of men;
For her the strong bow of his power he strung,
    And sent his arrows to the very den
Where grim Oppression held his bloody place
And gloated o'er the mis'ries of a race.

And he was no soft-tongued apologist;
    He spoke straightforward, fearlessly uncowed;
The sunlight of his truth dispelled the mist,
    And set in bold relief each dark-hued cloud;
To sin and crime he gave their proper hue,
And hurled at evil what was evil's due.

Through good and ill report he cleaved his way
    Right onward, with his face set toward the
      heights,
Nor feared to face the foeman's dread array, —
    The lash of scorn, the sting of petty spites.
He dared the lightning in the lightning's track,
And answered thunder with his thunder back.

Lyrics of Lowly Life.

When men maligned him, and their torrent
          wrath
    In furious imprecations o'er him broke,
He kept his counsel as he kept his path ;
    'T was for his race, not for himself, he spoke.
He knew the import of his Master's call,
And felt himself too mighty to be small.

No miser in the good he held was he, —
    His kindness followed his horizon's rim.
His heart, his talents, and his hands were free
    To all who truly needed aught of him.
Where poverty and ignorance were rife,
He gave his bounty as he gave his life.

The place and cause that first aroused his might
    Still proved its power until his latest day.
In Freedom's lists and for the aid of Right
    Still in the foremost rank he waged the fray ;
Wrong lived ; his occupation was not gone.
He died in action with his armor on !

We weep for him, but we have touched his hand,
    And felt the magic of his presence nigh,

The current that he sent throughout the land,
  The kindling spirit of his battle-cry.
O'er all that holds us we shall triumph yet,
And place our banner where his hopes were set !

Oh, Douglass, thou hast passed beyond the shore,
  But still thy voice is ringing o'er the gale !
Thou 'st taught thy race how high her hopes may
      soar,
  And bade her seek the heights, nor faint, nor
      fail.
She will not fail, she heeds thy stirring cry,
She knows thy guardian spirit will be nigh,
And, rising from beneath the chast'ning rod,
She stretches out her bleeding hands to God !

LIFE.

A CRUST of bread and a corner to sleep in,
    A minute to smile and an hour to weep in,
A pint of joy to a peck of trouble,
And never a laugh but the moans come double ;
    And that is life !

11

Lyrics of Lowly Life.

A crust and a corner that love makes precious,
With the smile to warm and the tears to re-
        fresh us;
And joy seems sweeter when cares come after,
And a moan is the finest of foils for laughter;
            And that is life!

THE LESSON.

MY cot was down by a cypress grove,
        And I sat by my window the whole
            night long,
And heard well up from the deep dark wood
    A mocking-bird's passionate song.

And I thought of myself so sad and lone,
    And my life's cold winter that knew no
        spring;
Of my mind so weary and sick and wild,
    Of my heart too sad to sing.

But e'en as I listened the mock-bird's song,
    A thought stole into my saddened heart,
And I said, " I can cheer some other soul
    By a carol's simple art."

12

Lyrics of Lowly Life.

For oft from the darkness of hearts and lives
    Come songs that brim with joy and light,
As out of the gloom of the cypress grove
    The mocking-bird sings at night.

So I sang a lay for a brother's ear
    In a strain to soothe his bleeding heart,
And he smiled at the sound of my voice and
        lyre,
    Though mine was a feeble art.

But at his smile I smiled in turn,
    And into my soul there came a ray:
In trying to soothe another's woes
    Mine own had passed away.

THE RISING OF THE STORM.

THE lake's dark breast
        Is all unrest,
It heaves with a sob and a sigh.
    Like a tremulous bird,
    From its slumber stirred,
The moon is a-tilt in the sky.

Lyrics of Lowly Life.

From the silent deep
    The waters sweep,
But faint on the cold white stones,
    And the wavelets fly
    With a plaintive cry
O'er the old earth's bare, bleak bones.

And the spray upsprings
    On its ghost-white wings,
And tosses a kiss at the stars ;
    While a water-sprite,
    In sea-pearls dight,
Hums a sea-hymn's solemn bars.

Far out in the night,
    On the wavering sight
I see a dark hull loom ;
    And its light on high,
    Like a Cyclops' eye,
Shines out through the mist and gloom.

Now the winds well up
    From the earth's deep cup,

Lyrics of Lowly Life.

And fall on the sea and shore,
  And against the pier
  The waters rear
And break with a sullen roar.

  Up comes the gale,
  And the mist-wrought veil
Gives way to the lightning's glare,
  And the cloud-drifts fall,
  A sombre pall,
O'er water, earth, and air.

  The storm-king flies,
  His whip he plics,
And bellows down the wind.
  The lightning rash
  With blinding flash
Comes pricking on behind.

  Rise, waters, rise,
  And taunt the skies
With your swift-flitting form.
  Sweep, wild winds, sweep,

And tear the deep
To atoms in the storm.

And the waters leapt,
And the wild winds swept,
And blew out the moon in the sky,
And I laughed with glee,
It was joy to me
As the storm went raging by !

SUNSET.

THE river sleeps beneath the sky,
   And clasps the shadows to its breast ;
The crescent moon shines dim on high ;
   And in the lately radiant west
      The gold is fading into gray.
      Now stills the lark his festive lay,
      And mourns with me the dying day.

While in the south the first faint star
   Lifts to the night its silver face,
And twinkles to the moon afar
   Across the heaven's graying space,

Lyrics of Lowly Life.

Low murmurs reach me from the town,
As Day puts on her sombre crown,
And shakes her mantle darkly down.

THE OLD APPLE-TREE.

THERE 's a memory keeps a-runnin'
  Through my weary head to-night,
An' I see a picture dancin'
  In the fire-flames' ruddy light;
'T is the picture of an orchard
  Wrapped in autumn's purple haze,
With the tender light about it
  That I loved in other days.
An' a-standin' in a corner
  Once again I seem to see
The verdant leaves an' branches
  Of an old apple-tree.

You perhaps would call it ugly,
  An' I don't know but it 's so,
When you look the tree all over
  Unadorned by memory's glow;

17

Lyrics of Lowly Life.

For its boughs are gnarled an' crooked,
　　An' its leaves are gettin' thin,
An' the apples of its bearin'
　　Would n't fill so large a bin
As they used to.　But I tell you,
　　When it comes to pleasin' me,
It 's the dearest in the orchard, —
　　Is that old apple-tree.

I would hide within its shelter,
　　Settlin' in some cosy nook,
Where no calls nor threats could stir me
　　From the pages o' my book.
Oh, that quiet, sweet seclusion
　　In its fulness passeth words !
It was deeper than the deepest
　　That my sanctum now affords.
Why, the jaybirds an' the robins,
　　They was hand in glove with me,
As they winked at me an' warbled
　　In that old apple-tree.

It was on its sturdy branches
　　That in summers long ago

Lyrics of Lowly Life.

I would tie my swing an' dangle
   In contentment to an' fro,
Idly dreamin' childish fancies,
   Buildin' castles in the air,
Makin' o' myself a hero
   Of romances rich an' rare.
I kin shet my eyes an' see it
   Jest as plain as plain kin be,
That same old swing a-danglin'
   To the old apple-tree.

There 's a rustic seat beneath it
   That I never kin forget.
It 's the place where me an' Hallie —
   Little sweetheart — used to set,
When we 'd wander to the orchard
   So 's no listenin' ones could hear
As I whispered sugared nonsense
   Into her little willin' ear.
Now my gray old wife is Hallie,
   An' I 'm grayer still than she,
But I 'll not forget our courtin'
   'Neath the old apple-tree.

19

Lyrics of Lowly Life.

Life for us ain't all been summer,
  But I guess we 've had our share
Of its flittin' joys an' pleasures,
  An' a sprinklin' of its care.
Oft the skies have smiled upon us;
  Then again we 've seen 'em frown,
Though our load was ne'er so heavy
  That we longed to lay it down.
But when death does come a-callin',
  This my last request shall be, —
That they 'll bury me an' Hallie
  'Neath the old apple-tree.

A PRAYER.

O LORD, the hard-won miles
    Have worn my stumbling feet:
Oh, soothe me with thy smiles,
    And make my life complete.

The thorns were thick and keen
    Where'er I trembling trod;
The way was long between
    My wounded feet and God.

Lyrics of Lowly Life.

Where healing waters flow
　Do thou my footsteps lead.
My heart is aching so ;
　Thy gracious balm I need.

PASSION AND LOVE.

A MAIDEN wept and, as a comforter,
　　Came one who cried, " I love thee,"
　　　and he seized
Her in his arms and kissed her with hot breath,
That dried the tears upon her flaming cheeks.
While evermore his boldly blazing eye
Burned into hers ; but she uncomforted
Shrank from his arms and only wept the more.

Then one came and gazed mutely in her face
With wide and wistful eyes ; but still aloof
He held himself ; as with a reverent fear,
As one who knows some sacred presence nigh.
And as she wept he mingled tear with tear,
That cheered her soul like dew a dusty flower, —
Until she smiled, approached, and touched his
　　hand !

Lyrics of Lowly Life.

THE SEEDLING.

A S a quiet little seedling
    Lay within its darksome bed,
To itself it fell a-talking,
    And this is what it said :

" I am not so very robust,
    But I 'll do the best I can ; "
And the seedling from that moment
    Its work of life began.

So it pushed a little leaflet
    Up into the light of day,
To examine the surroundings
    And show the rest the way.

The leaflet liked the prospect,
    So it called its brother, Stem ;
Then two other leaflets heard it,
    And quickly followed them.

To be sure, the haste and hurry
    Made the seedling sweat and pant ;

22

But almost before it knew it
    It found itself a plant.

The sunshine poured upon it,
    And the clouds they gave a shower;
And the little plant kept growing
    Till it found itself a flower.

Little folks, be like the seedling,
    Always do the best you can;
Every child must share life's labor
    Just as well as every man.

And the sun and showers will help you
    Through the lonesome, struggling hours,
Till you raise to light and beauty
    Virtue's fair, unfading flowers.

PROMISE.

I GREW a rose within a garden fair,
    And, tending it with more than loving care,
I thought how, with the glory of its bloom,
I should the darkness of my life illume;

And, watching, ever smiled to see the lusty bud
Drink freely in the summer sun to tinct its
blood.

My rose began to open, and its hue
Was sweet to me as to it sun and dew;
I watched it taking on its ruddy flame
Until the day of perfect blooming came,
Then hasted I with smiles to find it blushing
red —
Too late! Some thoughtless child had plucked
my rose and fled!

FULFILMENT.

I GREW a rose once more to please mine eyes.
All things to aid it — dew, sun, wind, fair
skies —
Were kindly; and to shield it from despoil,
I fenced it safely in with grateful toil.
No other hand than mine shall pluck this
flower, said I,
And I was jealous of the bee that hovered nigh.

24

Lyrics of Lowly Life.

It grew for days; I stood hour after hour
To watch the slow unfolding of the flower,
And then I did not leave its side at all,
Lest some mischance my flower should befall.
At last, oh joy! the central petals burst apart.
It blossomed — but, alas! a worm was at its
    heart!

SONG.

MY heart to thy heart,
    My hand to thine;
My lips to thy lips,
    Kisses are wine
Brewed for the lover in sunshine and shade;
Let me drink deep, then, my African maid.

    Lily to lily,
      Rose unto rose;
    My love to thy love
      Tenderly grows.
Rend not the oak and the ivy in twain,
Nor the swart maid from her swarthier swain.

25

Lyrics of Lowly Life.

AN ANTE-BELLUM SERMON.

WE is gathahed hyeah, my brothahs,
   In dis howlin' wildaness,
Fu' to speak some words of comfo't
   To each othah in distress.
An' we chooses fu' ouah subjic'
   Dis — we 'll 'splain it by an' by;
"An' de Lawd said, ' Moses, Moses,'
   An' de man said, ' Hyeah am I.'"

Now ole Pher'oh, down in Egypt,
   Was de wuss man evah bo'n,
An' he had de Hebrew chillun
   Down dah wukin' in his co'n;
'T well de Lawd got tiahed o' his foolin',
   An' sez he: "I 'll let him know —
Look hyeah, Moses, go tell Pher'oh
   Fu' to let dem chillun go."

" An' ef he refuse to do it,
   I will make him rue de houah,

26

Lyrics of Lowly Life.

Fu' I 'll empty down on Egypt
    All de vials of my powah."
Yes, he did — an' Pher'oh's ahmy
    Was n't wuth a ha'f a dime ;
Fu' de Lawd will he'p his chillun,
    You kin trust him evah time.

An' yo' enemies may 'sail you
    In de back an' in de front ;
But de Lawd is all aroun' you,
    Fu' to ba' de battle's brunt.
Dey kin fo'ge yo' chains an' shackles
    F'om de mountains to de sea ;
But de Lawd will sen' some Moses
    Fu' to set his chillun free.

An' de lan' shall hyeah his thundah,
    Lak a blas' f'om Gab'el's ho'n,
Fu' de Lawd of hosts is mighty
    When he girds his ahmor on.
But fu' feah some one mistakes me,
    I will pause right hyeah to say,
Dat I 'm still a-preachin' ancient,
    I ain't talkin' 'bout to-day.

27

Lyrics of Lowly Life.

But I tell you, fellah christuns,
   Things 'll happen mighty strange ;
Now, de Lawd done dis fu' Isrul,
   An' his ways don't nevah change,
An' de love he showed to Isrul
   Was n't all on Isrul spent ;
Now don't run an' tell yo' mastahs
   Dat I 's preachin' discontent.

'Cause I is n't ; I 'se a-judgin'
   Bible people by deir ac's ;
I 'se a-givin' you de Scriptuah,
   I 'se a-handin' you de fac's.
Cose ole Pher'oh b'lieved in slav'ry,
   But de Lawd he let him see,
Dat de people he put bref in, —
   Evah mothah's son was free.

An' dahs othahs thinks lak Pher'oh,
   But dey calls de Scriptuah liar,
Fu' de Bible says " a servant
   Is a-worthy of his hire."
An' you cain't git roun' nor thoo dat,
   An' you cain't git ovah it,

Lyrics of Lowly Life.

Fu' whatevah place you git in,
  Dis hyeah Bible too 'll fit.

So you see de Lawd's intention,
  Evah sence de worl' began,
Was dat His almighty freedom
  Should belong to evah man,
But I think it would be bettah,
  Ef I 'd pause agin to say,
Dat I 'm talkin' 'bout ouah freedom
  In a Bibleistic way.

But de Moses is a-comin',
  An' he 's comin', suah and fas'
We kin hyeah his feet a-trompin',
  We kin hyeah his trumpit blas'.
But I want to wa'n you people,
  Don't you git too brigity;
An' don't you git to braggin'
  'Bout dese things, you wait an' see.

But when Moses wif his powah
  Comes an' sets us chillun free,

Lyrics of Lowly Life.

We will praise de gracious Mastah
    Dat has gin us liberty;
An' we 'll shout ouah halleluyahs,
    On dat mighty reck'nin' day,
When we 'se reco'nised ez citiz' —
    Huh uh!   Chillun, let us pray!

ODE TO ETHIOPIA.

O MOTHER Race! to thee I bring
    This pledge of faith unwavering,
  This tribute to thy glory.
I know the pangs which thou didst feel,
When Slavery crushed thee with its heel,
  With thy dear blood all gory.

Sad days were those — ah, sad indeed!
But through the land the fruitful seed
  Of better times was growing.
The plant of freedom upward sprung,
And spread its leaves so fresh and young —
  Its blossoms now are blowing.

30

Lyrics of Lowly Life.

On every hand in this fair land,
Proud Ethiope's swarthy children stand
    Beside their fairer neighbor;
The forests flee before their stroke,
Their hammers ring, their forges smoke, —
    They stir in honest labour.

They tread the fields where honour calls;
Their voices sound through senate halls
    In majesty and power.
To right they cling; the hymns they sing
Up to the skies in beauty ring,
    And bolder grow each hour.

Be proud, my Race, in mind and soul;
Thy name is writ on Glory's scroll
    In characters of fire.
High 'mid the clouds of Fame's bright sky
Thy banner's blazoned folds now fly,
    And truth shall lift them higher.

Thou hast the right to noble pride,
Whose spotless robes were purified

Lyrics of Lowly Life.

By blood's severe baptism.
Upon thy brow the cross was laid,
And labour's painful sweat-beads made
   A consecrating chrism.

No other race, or white or black,
When bound as thou wert, to the rack,
   So seldom stooped to grieving ;
No other race, when free again,
Forgot the past and proved them men
   So noble in forgiving.

Go on and up !   Our souls and eyes
Shall follow thy continuous rise ;
   Our ears shall list thy story
From bards who from thy root shall spring,
And proudly tune their lyres to sing
   Of Ethiopia's glory.

Lyrics of Lowly Life.

THE CORN-STALK FIDDLE.

WHEN the corn's all cut and the bright
    stalks shine
Like the burnished spears of a field of gold;
When the field-mice rich on the nubbins dine,
    And the frost comes white and the wind
      blows cold;
Then it's heigho! fellows and hi-diddle-diddle,
For the time is ripe for the corn-stalk fiddle.

And you take a stalk that is straight and long,
    With an expert eye to its worthy points,
And you think of the bubbling strains of song
    That are bound between its pithy joints —
Then you cut out strings, with a bridge in the
      middle,
With a corn-stalk bow for a corn-stalk fiddle.

Then the strains that grow as you draw the bow
    O'er the yielding strings with a practised
      hand!

Lyrics of Lowly Life.

And the music's flow never loud but low
   Is the concert note of a fairy band.
Oh, your dainty songs are a misty riddle
To the simple sweets of the corn-stalk fiddle.

When the eve comes on, and our work is done,
   And the sun drops down with a tender glance,
With their hearts all prime for the harmless fun,
    Come the neighbor girls for the evening's
      dance,
And they wait for the well-known twist and
      twiddle —
More time than tune — from the corn-stalk
      fiddle.

Then brother Jabez takes the bow,
   While Ned stands off with Susan Bland,
Then Henry stops by Milly Snow,
   And John takes Nellie Jones's hand,
While I pair off with Mandy Biddle,
And scrape, scrape, scrape goes the corn-stalk
      fiddle.

Lyrics of Lowly Life.

"Salute your partners," comes the call,
　" All join hands and circle round,"
" Grand train back," and " Balance all,"
　Footsteps lightly spurn the ground.
" Take your lady and balance down the middle "
To the merry strains of the corn-stalk fiddle.

So the night goes on and the dance is o'er,
　And the merry girls are homeward gone,
But I see it all in my sleep once more,
　And I dream till the very break of dawn
Of an impish dance on a red-hot griddle
To the screech and scrape of a corn-stalk
　　　fiddle.

THE MASTER-PLAYER.

AN old, worn harp that had been played
　　Till all its strings were loose and frayed,
Joy, Hate, and Fear, each one essayed,
To play.　But each in turn had found
No sweet responsiveness of sound.

Lyrics of Lowly Life.

Then Love the Master-Player came
With heaving breast and eyes aflame;
The Harp he took all undismayed,
Smote on its strings, still strange to song,
And brought forth music sweet and strong.

THE MYSTERY.

I WAS not; now I am — a few days hence
    I shall not be; I fain would look before
And after, but can neither do; some Power
Or lack of power says "no" to all I would.
I stand upon a wide and sunless plain,
Nor chart nor steel to guide my steps aright.
Whene'er, o'ercoming fear, I dare to move,
I grope without direction and by chance.
Some feign to hear a voice and feel a hand
That draws them ever upward thro' the gloom.
But I — I hear no voice and touch no hand,
Tho' oft thro' silence infinite I list,

And strain my hearing to supernal sounds;
Tho' oft thro' fateful darkness do I reach,
And stretch my hand to find that other hand.
I question of th' eternal bending skies
That seem to neighbor with the novice earth;
But they roll on, and daily shut their eyes
On me, as I one day shall do on them,
And tell me not the secret that I ask.

NOT THEY WHO SOAR.

NOT they who soar, but they who plod
    Their rugged way, unhelped, to God
Are heroes; they who higher fare,
And, flying, fan the upper air,
Miss all the toil that hugs the sod.
'Tis they whose backs have felt the rod,
Whose feet have pressed the path unshod,
May smile upon defeated care,
    Not they who soar.

37

High up there are no thorns to prod,
Nor boulders lurking 'neath the clod
To turn the keenness of the share,
For flight is ever free and rare ;
But heroes they the soil who 've trod,
    Not they who soar !

WHITTIER.

NOT o'er thy dust let there be spent
    The gush of maudlin sentiment ;
Such drift as that is not for thee,
Whose life and deeds and songs agree,
Sublime in their simplicity.

Nor shall the sorrowing tear be shed.
O singer sweet, thou art not dead !
In spite of time's malignant chill,
With living fire thy songs shall thrill,
And men shall say, " He liveth still ! "

Great poets never die, for Earth
Doth count their lives of too great worth

Lyrics of Lowly Life.

To lose them from her treasured store;
So shalt thou live for evermore —
Though far thy form from mortal ken —
Deep in the hearts and minds of men.

TWO SONGS.

A BEE that was searching for sweets one
    day
Through the gate of a rose garden happened to
    stray.
In the heart of a rose he hid away,
And forgot in his bliss the light of day,
As sipping his honey he buzzed in song;
Though day was waning, he lingered long,

    For the rose was sweet, so sweet.

A robin sits pluming his ruddy breast,
And a madrigal sings to his love in her nest:
"Oh, the skies they are blue, the fields are
    green,
And the birds in your nest will soon be seen!"

Lyrics of Lowly Life.

She hangs on his words with a thrill of love,
And chirps to him as he sits above,
    For the song is sweet, so sweet.

A maiden was out on a summer's day
With the winds and the waves and the flowers
    at play;
And she met with a youth of gentle air,
With the light of the sunshine on his hair.
Together they wandered the flowers among;
They loved, and loving they lingered long,
    For to love is sweet, so sweet.

―――

BIRD of my lady's bower,
   Sing her a song;
Tell her that every hour,
   All the day long,
Thoughts of her come to me,
   Filling my brain
With the warm ecstasy
   Of love's refrain.

Lyrics of Lowly Life.

Little bird ! happy bird !
   Being so near,
Where e'en her slightest word
   Thou mayest hear,
Seeing her glancing eyes,
   Sheen of her hair,
Thou art in paradise, —
   Would I were there.

I am so far away,
   Thou art so near ;
Plead with her, birdling gay,
   Plead with my dear.
Rich be thy recompense,
   Fine be thy fee,
If through thine eloquence
   She hearken me.

A BANJO SONG.

OH, dere 's lots o' keer an' trouble
    In dis world to swaller down;
An' ol' Sorrer 's purty lively
    In her way o' gittin' roun'.
Yet dere 's times when I furgit 'em, —
    Aches an' pains an' troubles all, —
An' it 's when I tek at ebenin'
    My ol' banjo f'om de wall.

'Bout de time dat night is fallin'
    An' my daily wu'k is done,
An' above de shady hilltops
    I kin see de settin' sun;
When de quiet, restful shadders
    Is beginnin' jes' to fall, —
Den I take de little banjo
    F'om its place upon de wall.

42

Lyrics of Lowly Life.

Den my fam'ly gadders roun' me
  In de fadin' o' de light,
Ez I strike de strings to try 'em
  Ef dey all is tuned er-right.
An' it seems we 're so nigh heaben
  We kin hyeah de angels sing
When de music o' dat banjo
  Sets my cabin all er-ring.

An' my wife an' all de othahs, —
  Male an' female, small an' big, —
Even up to gray-haired granny,
  Seem jes' boun' to do a jig;
'Twell I change de style o' music,
  Change de movement an' de time,
An' de ringin' little banjo
  Plays an ol' hea't-feelin' hime.

An' somehow my th'oat gits choky,
  An' a lump keeps tryin' to rise
Lak it wan'ed to ketch de water
  Dat was flowin' to my eyes;

Lyrics of Lowly Life.

An' I feel dat I could sorter
    Knock de socks clean off o' sin
Ez I hyeah my po' ol' granny
    Wif huh tremblin' voice jine in.

Den we all th'ow in our voices
    Fu' to he'p de chune out too,
Lak a big camp-meetin' choiry
    Tryin' to sing a mou'nah th'oo.
An' our th'oahts let out de music,
    Sweet an' solemn, loud an' free,
'Twell de raftahs o' my cabin
    Echo wif de melody.

Oh, de music o' de banjo,
    Quick an' deb'lish, solemn, slow,
Is de greates' joy an' solace
    Dat a weary slave kin know !
So jes' let me hyeah it ringin',
    Dough de chune be po' an' rough,
It 's a pleasure ; an' de pleasures
    O' dis life is few enough.

44

Lyrics of Lowly Life.

Now, de blessed little angels
    Up in heaben, we are told,
Don't do nothin' all dere lifetime
    'Ceptin' play on ha'ps o' gold.
Now I think heaben 'd be mo' homelike
    Ef we 'd hyeah some music fall
F'om a real ol'-fashioned banjo,
    Like dat one upon de wall.

LONGING.

IF you could sit with me beside the sea
        to-day,
And whisper with me sweetest dreamings o'er
        and o'er ;
I think I should not find the clouds so dim and
        gray,
And not so loud the waves complaining at the
        shore.

If you could sit with me upon the shore to-day,
And hold my hand in yours as in the days of old,

Lyrics of Lowly Life.

I think I should not mind the chill baptismal
    spray,
Nor find my hand and heart and all the world
    so cold.

If you could walk with me upon the strand to-day,
And tell me that my longing love had won your
    own,
I think all my sad thoughts would then be put
    away,
And I could give back laughter for the Ocean's
    moan !

THE PATH.

THERE are no beaten paths to Glory's
    height,
There are no rules to compass greatness known;
Each for himself must cleave a path alone,
And press his own way forward in the fight.
Smooth is the way to ease and calm delight,
And soft the road Sloth chooseth for her own ;
But he who craves the flower of life full-blown,

Lyrics of Lowly Life.

Must struggle up in all his armor dight !
What though the burden bear him sorely down
And crush to dust the mountain of his pride,
Oh, then, with strong heart let him still abide ;
For rugged is the roadway to renown,
Nor may he hope to gain the envied crown
Till he hath thrust the looming rocks aside.

THE LAWYERS' WAYS.

I 'VE been list'nin' to them lawyers
   In the court house up the street,
An' I 've come to the conclusion
   That I 'm most completely beat.
Fust one feller riz to argy,
   An' he boldly waded in
As he dressed the tremblin' pris'ner
   In a coat o' deep-dyed sin.

Why, he painted him all over
   In a hue o' blackest crime,
An' he smeared his reputation
   With the thickest kind o' grime,

Lyrics of Lowly Life.

Tell I found myself a-wond'rin',
  In a misty way and dim,
How the Lord had come to fashion
  Sich an awful man as him.

Then the other lawyer started,
  An', with brimmin', tearful eyes,
Said his client was a martyr
  That was brought to sacrifice.
An' he give to that same pris'ner
  Every blessed human grace,
Tell I saw the light o' virtue
  Fairly shinin' from his face.

Then I own 'at I was puzzled
  How sich things could rightly be ;
An' this aggervatin' question
  Seems to keep a-puzzlin' me.
So, will some one please inform me,
  An' this mystery unroll —
How an angel an' a devil
  Can persess the self-same soul?

ODE FOR MEMORIAL DAY.

DONE are the toils and the wearisome
marches,
    Done is the summons of bugle and drum.
Softly and sweetly the sky overarches,
    Shelt'ring a land where Rebellion is dumb.
Dark were the days of the country's derange-
ment,
    Sad were the hours when the conflict was on,
But through the gloom of fraternal estrangement
    God sent his light, and we welcome the dawn.
O'er the expanse of our mighty dominions,
    Sweeping away to the uttermost parts,
Peace, the wide-flying, on untiring pinions,
    Bringeth her message of joy to our hearts.

Ah, but this joy which our minds cannot measure,
    What did it cost for our fathers to gain !
Bought at the price of the heart's dearest treasure,
    Born out of travail and sorrow and pain ;

Lyrics of Lowly Life.

Born in the battle where fleet Death was flying,
  Slaying with sabre-stroke bloody and fell;
Born where the heroes and martyrs were dying,
  Torn by the fury of bullet and shell.
Ah, but the day is past: silent the rattle,
  And the confusion that followed the fight.
Peace to the heroes who died in the battle,
  Martyrs to truth and the crowning of Right!

Out of the blood of a conflict fraternal,
  Out of the dust and the dimness of death,
Burst into blossoms of glory eternal
    Flowers that sweeten the world with their
        breath.
Flowers of charity, peace, and devotion
  Bloom in the hearts that are empty of strife;
Love that is boundless and broad as the ocean
  Leaps into beauty and fulness of life.
So, with the singing of pæans and chorals,
  And with the flag flashing high in the sun,
Place on the graves of our heroes the laurels
  Which their unfaltering valor has won!

PREMONITION.

DEAR heart, good-night !
    Nay, list awhile that sweet voice
        singing
When the world is all so bright,
And the sound of song sets the heart a-ringing,
  Oh, love, it is not right —
    Not then to say, " Good-night."

    Dear heart, good-night !
The late winds in the lake weeds shiver,
  And the spray flies cold and white.
And the voice that sings gives a telltale quiver —
  " Ah, yes, the world is bright,
    But, dearest heart, good-night ! "

    Dear heart, good-night !
And do not longer seek to hold me !
  For my soul is in affright
As the fearful glooms in their pall enfold me.
  See him who sang how white
    And still ; so, dear, good-night.

Lyrics of Lowly Life.

Dear heart, good-night !
Thy hand I 'll press no more forever,
    And mine eyes shall lose the light ;
For the great white wraith by the winding river
    Shall check my steps with might.
        So, dear, good-night, good-night !

RETROSPECTION.

WHEN you and I were young, the days
        Were filled with scent of pink and rose,
    And full of joy from dawn till close,
From morning's mist till evening's haze.
    And when the robin sung his song
    The verdant woodland ways along,
        We whistled louder than he sung.
And school was joy, and work was sport
For which the hours were all too short,
    When you and I were young, my boy,
        When you and I were young.

52

Lyrics of Lowly Life.

When you and I were young, the woods
  Brimmed bravely o'er with every joy
  To charm the happy-hearted boy.
The quail turned out her timid broods;
  The prickly copse, a hostess fine,
  Held high black cups of harmless wine;
    And low the laden grape-vine swung
With beads of night-kissed amethyst
Where buzzing lovers held their tryst,
  When you and I were young, my boy,
    When you and I were young.

When you and I were young, the cool
  And fresh wind fanned our fevered brows
  When tumbling o'er the scented mows,
Or stripping by the dimpling pool,
  Sedge-fringed about its shimmering face,
  Save where we 'd worn an ent'ring place.
    How with our shouts the calm banks rung!
How flashed the spray as we plunged in, —
Pure gems that never caused a sin!
  When you and I were young, my boy,
    When you and I were young.

Lyrics of Lowly Life.

When you and I were young, we heard
   All sounds of Nature with delight, —
   The whirr of wing in sudden flight,
The chirping of the baby-bird.
   The columbine's red bells were rung ;
   The locust's vested chorus sung ;
     While every wind his zithern strung
To high and holy-sounding keys,
And played sonatas in the trees —
   When you and I were young, my boy,
     When you and I were young.

When you and I were young, we knew
   To shout and laugh, to work and play,
   And night was partner to the day
In all our joys.   So swift time flew
   On silent wings that, ere we wist,
   The fleeting years had fled unmissed ;
     And from our hearts this cry was wrung —
To fill with fond regret and tears
The days of our remaining years —
   " When you and I were young, my boy,
     When you and I were young."

54

Lyrics of Lowly Life.

UNEXPRESSED.

DEEP in my heart that aches with the re-
pression,
  And strives with plenitude of bitter pain,
There lives a thought that clamors for ex-
pression,
  And spends its undelivered force in vain.

What boots it that some other may have
    thought it?
  The right of thoughts' expression is divine;
The price of pain I pay for it has bought it,
  I care not who lays claim to it — 't is mine !

And yet not mine until it be delivered;
  The manner of its birth shall prove the test.
Alas, alas, my rock of pride is shivered —
  I beat my brow — the thought still unex-
pressed.

SONG OF SUMMER.

DIS is gospel weathah sho' —
　　Hills is sawt o' hazy.
Meddahs level ez a flo'
　　Callin' to de lazy.
Sky all white wif streaks o' blue,
　　Sunshine softly gleamin',
D'ain't no wuk hit's right to do,
　　Nothin' 's right but dreamin'.

Dreamin' by de rivah side
　　Wif de watahs glist'nin',
Feelin' good an' satisfied
　　Ez you lay a-list'nin'
To the little nakid boys
　　Splashin' in de watah,
Hollerin' fu' to spress deir joys
　　Jes' lak youngsters ought to.

56

Lyrics of Lowly Life.

Squir'l a-tippin' on his toes,
  So 's to hide an' view you ;
Whole flocks o' camp-meetin' crows
  Shoutin' hallelujah.
Peckahwood erpon de tree
  Tappin' lak a hammah ;
Jaybird chattin' wif a bee,
  Tryin' to teach him grammah.

Breeze is blowin' wif perfume,
  Jes' enough to tease you ;
Hollyhocks is all in bloom,
  Smellin' fu' to please you.
Go 'way, folks, an' let me 'lone,
  Times is gettin' dearah —
Summah 's settin' on de th'one,
  An' I 'm a-layin' neah huh !

Lyrics of Lowly Life.

SPRING SONG.

A BLUE–BELL springs upon the ledge,
   A lark sits singing in the hedge ;
Sweet perfumes scent the balmy air,
And life is brimming everywhere.
What lark and breeze and bluebird sing,
   Is Spring, Spring, Spring !

No more the air is sharp and cold ;
The planter wends across the wold,
And, glad, beneath the shining sky
We wander forth, my love and I.
And ever in our hearts doth ring
   This song of Spring, Spring !

For life is life and love is love,
'Twixt maid and man or dove and dove.
Life may be short, life may be long,
But love will come, and to its song
Shall this refrain for ever cling
   Of Spring, Spring, Spring !

TO LOUISE.

OH, the poets may sing of their Lady Irenes,
    And may rave in their rhymes about
        wonderful queens;
But I throw my poetical wings to the breeze,
And soar in a song to my Lady Louise.
A sweet little maid, who is dearer, I ween,
Than any fair duchess, or even a queen.
When speaking of her I can't plod in my
    prose,
For she 's the wee lassie who gave me a rose.

Since poets, from seeing a lady's lip curled,
Have written fair verse that has sweetened the
    world;
Why, then, should not I give the space of an
    hour
To making a song in return for a flower?

59

Lyrics of Lowly Life.

I have found in my life — it has not been so
    long —
There are too few of flowers — too little of song.
So out of that blossom, this lay of mine grows,
For the dear little lady who gave me the rose.

I thank God for innocence, dearer than Art,
That lights on a by-way which leads to the
    heart,
And led by an impulse no less than divine,
Walks into the temple and sits at the shrine.
I would rather pluck daisies that grow in the
    wild,
Or take one simple rose from the hand of a
    child,
Than to breathe the rich fragrance of flowers
    that bide
In the gardens of luxury, passion, and pride.

I know not, my wee one, how came you to know
Which way to my heart was the right way to go ;
Unless in your purity, soul-clean and clear,
God whispers his messages into your ear.

Lyrics of Lowly Life.

You have now had my song, let me end with a
    prayer
That your life may be always sweet, happy, and
    fair ;
That your joys may be many, and absent your
    woes,
O dear little lady who gave me the rose !

THE RIVALS.

'TWAS three an' thirty year ago,
    When I was ruther young, you know,
I had my last an' only fight
About a gal one summer night.
'T was me an' Zekel Johnson ; Zeke
'N' me 'd be'n spattin' 'bout a week,
Each of us tryin' his best to show
That he was Liza Jones's beau.
We could n't neither prove the thing,
Fur she was fur too sharp to fling
One over fur the other one
An' by so doin' stop the fun

Lyrics of Lowly Life.

That we chaps did n't have the sense
To see she got at our expense,
But that 's the way a feller does,
Fur boys is fools an' allus was.
An' when they 's females in the game
I reckon men 's about the same.
Well, Zeke an' me went on that way
An' fussed an' quarrelled day by day;
While Liza, mindin' not the fuss,
Jest kep' a-goin' with both of us,
Tell we pore chaps, that 's Zeke an' me,
Was jest plum mad with jealousy.
Well, fur a time we kep' our places,
An' only showed by frownin' faces
An' looks 'at well our meanin' boded
How full o' fight we both was loaded.
At last it come, the thing broke out,
An' this is how it come about.
One night ('t was fair, you 'll all agree)
I got Eliza's company,
An' leavin' Zekel in the lurch,
Went trottin' off with her to church.
An' jest as we had took our seat

Lyrics of Lowly Life.

(Eliza lookin' fair an' sweet),
Why, I jest could n't help but grin
When Zekel come a-bouncin' in
As furious as the law allows.
He 'd jest be'n up to Liza's house,
To find her gone, then come to church
To have this end put to his search.
I guess I laffed that meetin' through,
An' not a mortal word I knew
Of what the preacher preached er read
Er what the choir sung er said.
Fur every time I 'd turn my head
I could n't skeercely help but see
'At Zekel had his eye on me.
An' he 'ud sort o' turn an' twist
An' grind his teeth an' shake his fist.
I laughed, fur la ! the hull church seen us,
An' knowed that suthin' was between us.
Well, meetin' out, we started hum,
I sorter feelin' what would come.
We 'd jest got out, when up stepped Zeke,
An' said, "Scuse me, I 'd like to speak
To you a minute."   "Cert," said I —

63

Lyrics of Lowly Life.

A-nudgin' Liza on the sly
An' laughin' in my sleeve with glee,
I asked her, please, to pardon me.
We walked away a step er two,
Jest to git out o' Liza's view,
An' then Zeke said, " I want to know
Ef you think you 're Eliza's beau,
An' 'at I 'm goin' to let her go
Hum with sich a chap as you? "
An' I said bold, " You bet I do."
Then Zekel, sneerin', said 'at he
Did n't want to hender me.
But then he 'lowed the gal was his
An' 'at he guessed he knowed his biz,
An' was n't feared o' all my kin
With all my friends an' chums throwed in.
Some other things he mentioned there
That no born man could no ways bear
Er think o' ca'mly tryin' to stan'
Ef Zeke had be'n the bigges' man
In town, an' not the leanest runt
'At time an' labor ever stunt.
An' so I let my fist go " bim,"

Lyrics of Lowly Life.

I thought I 'd mos' nigh finished him.
But Zekel did n't take it so.
He jest ducked down an' dodged my blow
An' then come back at me so hard,
I guess I must 'a' hurt the yard,
Er spilet the grass plot where I fell,
An' sakes alive it hurt me ; well,
It would n't be'n so bad, you see,
But he jest kep' a-hittin' me.
An' I hit back an' kicked an' pawed,
But 't seemed 't was mostly air I clawed,
While Zekel used his science well
A-makin' every motion tell.
He punched an' hit, why, goodness lands,
Seemed like he had a dozen hands.
Well, afterwhile they stopped the fuss,
An' some one kindly parted us.
All beat an' cuffed an' clawed an' scratched,
An' needin' both our faces patched,
Each started hum a different way ;
An' what o' Liza, do you say,
Why, Liza — little humbug — dern her,
Why, she 'd gone home with Hiram Turner.

Lyrics of Lowly Life.

THE LOVER AND THE MOON.

A LOVER whom duty called over the wave,
  With himself communed: " Will my
   love be true
If left to herself? Had I better not sue
Some friend to watch over her, good and grave?
  But my friend might fail in my need," he
   said,
  "And I return to find love dead.
  Since friendships fade like the flow'rs of June,
  I will leave her in charge of the stable moon."

Then he said to the moon: " O dear old moon,
  Who for years and years from thy throne above
  Hast nurtured and guarded young lovers and
   love,
My heart has but come to its waiting June,
  And the promise time of the budding vine;
  Oh, guard thee well this love of mine."
  And he harked him then while all was still,
  And the pale moon answered and said, " I will."

Lyrics of Lowly Life.

And he sailed in his ship o'er many seas,
   And he wandered wide o'er strange far
      strands :
   In isles of the south and in Orient lands,
Where pestilence lurks in the breath of the
      breeze.
   But his star was high, so he braved the main,
   And sailed him blithely home again ;
   And with joy he bended his footsteps soon
   To learn of his love from the matron moon.

She sat as of yore, in her olden place,
   Serene as death, in her silver chair.
   A white rose gleamed in her whiter hair,
And the tint of a blush was on her face.
   At sight of the youth she sadly bowed
   And hid her face 'neath a gracious cloud.
   She faltered faint on the night's dim marge,
   But " How," spoke the youth, " have you
      kept your charge ? "

The moon was sad at a trust ill-kept ;
   The blush went out in her blanching cheek,

And her voice was timid and low and weak,
As she made her plea and sighed and wept.
 " Oh, another prayed and another plead,
 And I could n't resist," she answering said ;
 " But love still grows in the hearts of men :
 Go forth, dear youth, and love again."

But he turned him away from her proffered grace.
 " Thou art false, O moon, as the hearts of
  men,
 I will not, will not love again."
And he turned sheer 'round with a soul-sick
  face
 To the sea, and cried : " Sea, curse the moon,
 Who makes her vows and forgets so soon."
 And the awful sea with anger stirred,
 And his breast heaved hard as he lay and
  heard.

And ever the moon wept down in rain,
 And ever her sighs rose high in wind ;
 But the earth and sea were deaf and blind,
And she wept and sighed her griefs in vain.

And ever at night, when the storm is fierce,
The cries of a wraith through the thunders
    pierce ;
And the waves strain their awful hands on
    high
To tear the false moon from the sky.

CONSCIENCE AND REMORSE.

" GOOD–BYE," I said to my conscience —
    " Good-bye for aye and aye,"
And I put her hands off harshly,
    And turned my face away ;
And conscience smitten sorely
    Returned not from that day.

But a time came when my spirit
    Grew weary of its pace ;
And I cried : " Come back, my conscience ;
    I long to see thy face."
But conscience cried : " I cannot ;
    Remorse sits in my place."

69

Lyrics of Lowly Life.

IONE.

I.

AH, yes, 't is sweet still to remember,
  Though 't were less painful to forget;
For while my heart glows like an ember,
  Mine eyes with sorrow's drops are wet,
  And, oh, my heart is aching yet.
It is a law of mortal pain
  That old wounds, long accounted well,
  Beneath the memory's potent spell,
Will wake to life and bleed again.

So 't is with me; it might be better
  If I should turn no look behind, —
If I could curb my heart, and fetter
  From reminiscent gaze my mind,
  Or let my soul go blind — go blind!
But would I do it if I could?
  Nay! ease at such a price were spurned;
  For, since my love was once returned,
All that I suffer seemeth good.

Lyrics of Lowly Life.

I know, I know it is the fashion,
   When love has left some heart distressed,
To weight the air with wordful passion;
    But I am glad that in my breast
    I ever held so dear a guest.
Love does not come at every nod,
   Or every voice that calleth " hasten; "
   He seeketh out some heart to chasten,
And whips it, wailing, up to God!

Love is no random road wayfarer
   Who where he may must sip his glass.
Love is the King, the Purple-Wearer,
    Whose guard recks not of tree or grass
    To blaze the way that he may pass.
What if my heart be in the blast
   That heralds his triumphant way;
   Shall I repine, shall I not say:
" Rejoice, my heart, the King has passed! "

In life, each heart holds some sad story —
   The saddest ones are never told.
I, too, have dreamed of fame and glory,
   And viewed the future bright with gold;

Lyrics of Lowly Life.

But that is as a tale long told.
Mine eyes have lost their youthful flash,
  My cunning hand has lost its art;
  I am not old, but in my heart
The ember lies beneath the ash.

I loved! Why not? My heart was youthful,
  My mind was filled with healthy thought.
He doubts not whose own self is truthful,
  Doubt by dishonesty is taught;
  So loved I boldly, fearing naught.
I did not walk this lowly earth;
  Mine was a newer, higher sphere,
  Where youth was long and life was dear,
And all save love was little worth.

Her likeness! Would that I might limn it,
  As Love did, with enduring art;
Nor dust of days nor death may dim it,
  Where it lies graven on my heart,
  Of this sad fabric of my life a part.
I would that I might paint her now
  As I beheld her in that day,

Lyrics of Lowly Life.

Ere her first bloom had passed away,
  And left the lines upon her brow.

A face serene that, beaming brightly,
  Disarmed the hot sun's glances bold.
A foot that kissed the ground so lightly,
  He frowned in wrath and deemed her cold,
  But loved her still though he was old.
A form where every maiden grace
  Bloomed to perfection's richest flower, —
  The statued pose of conscious power,
Like lithe-limbed Dian's of the chase.

Beneath a brow too fair for frowning,
  Like moon-lit deeps that glass the skies
Till all the hosts above seem drowning,
  Looked forth her steadfast hazel eyes,
  With gaze serene and purely wise.
And over all, her tresses rare,
  Which, when, with his desire grown weak,
  The Night bent down to kiss her cheek,
Entrapped and held him captive there.

Lyrics of Lowly Life.

This was Ione ; a spirit finer
   Ne'er burned to ash its house of clay ;
A soul instinct with fire diviner
   Ne'er fled athwart the face of day,
   And tempted Time with earthly stay.
Her loveliness was not alone
   Of face and form and tresses' hue ;
   For aye a pure, high soul shone through
Her every act : this was Ione.

II.

'T was in the radiant summer weather,
   When God looked, smiling, from the sky ;
And we went wand'ring much together
   By wood and lane, Ione and I,
   Attracted by the subtle tie
Of common thoughts and common tastes,
   Of eyes whose vision saw the same,
   And freely granted beauty's claim
Where others found but worthless wastes.

We paused to hear the far bells ringing
   Across the distance, sweet and clear.

74

Lyrics of Lowly Life.

We listened to the wild bird's singing
   The song he meant for his mate's ear,
   And deemed our chance to do so dear.
We loved to watch the warrior Sun,
   With flaming shield and flaunting crest,
   Go striding down the gory West,
When Day's long fight was fought and won.

And life became a different story;
   Where'er I looked, I saw new light.
Earth's self assumed a greater glory,
   Mine eyes were cleared to fuller sight.
   Then first I saw the need and might
Of that fair band, the singing throng,
   Who, gifted with the skill divine,
   Take up the threads of life, spun fine,
And weave them into soulful song.

They sung for me, whose passion pressing
   My soul, found vent in song nor line.
They bore the burden of expressing
   All that I felt, with art's design,
   And every word of theirs was mine.

Lyrics of Lowly Life.

I read them to Ione, ofttimes,
  By hill and shore, beneath fair skies,
  And she looked deeply in mine eyes,
And knew my love spoke through their rhymes.

Her life was like the stream that floweth,
  And mine was like the waiting sea;
Her love was like the flower that bloweth,
  And mine was like the searching bee —
  I found her sweetness all for me.
God plied him in the mint of time,
  And coined for us a golden day,
  And rolled it ringing down life's way
With love's sweet music in its chime.

And God unclasped the Book of Ages,
  And laid it open to our sight;
Upon the dimness of its pages,
  So long consigned to rayless night,
  He shed the glory of his light.
We read them well, we read them long,
  And ever thrilling did we see
  That love ruled all humanity, —
The master passion, pure and strong.

Lyrics of Lowly Life.

III.

To-DAY my skies are bare and ashen,
    And bend on me without a beam.
Since love is held the master-passion,
    Its loss must be the pain supreme —
    And grinning Fate has wrecked my dream.
But pardon, dear departed Guest,
    I will not rant, I will not rail;
    For good the grain must feel the flail;
There are whom love has never blessed.

I had and have a younger brother,
    One whom I loved and love to-day
As never fond and doting mother
    Adored the babe who found its way
    From heavenly scenes into her day.
Oh, he was full of youth's new wine, —
    A man on life's ascending slope,
    Flushed with ambition, full of hope;
And every wish of his was mine.

A kingly youth; the way before him
    Was thronged with victories to be won;

77

Lyrics of Lowly Life.

So joyous, too, the heavens o'er him
    Were bright with an unchanging sun, —
    His days with rhyme were overrun.
Toil had not taught him Nature's prose,
    Tears had not dimmed his brilliant eyes,
    And sorrow had not made him wise ;
His life was in the budding rose.

I know not how I came to waken,
    Some instinct pricked my soul to sight ;
My heart by some vague thrill was shaken, —
    A thrill so true and yet so slight,
    I hardly deemed I read aright.
As when a sleeper, ign'rant why,
    Not knowing what mysterious hand
    Has called him out of slumberland,
Starts up to find some danger nigh.

Love is a guest that comes, unbidden,
    But, having come, asserts his right ;
He will not be repressed nor hidden.
    And so my brother's dawning plight
    Became uncovered to my sight.

Lyrics of Lowly Life.

Some sound-mote in his passing tone
  Caught in the meshes of my ear ;
  Some little glance, a shade too dear,
Betrayed the love he bore Ione.

What could I do?   He was my brother,
  And young, and full of hope and trust ;
I could not, dared not try to smother
  His flame, and turn his heart to dust.
  I knew how oft life gives a crust
To starving men who cry for bread ;
  But he was young, so few his days,
  He had not learned the great world's ways,
Nor Disappointment's volumes read.

However fair and rich the booty,
  I could not make his loss my gain.
For love is dear, but dearer, duty,
  And here my way was clear and plain.
  I saw how I could save him pain.
And so, with all my day grown dim,
  That this loved brother's sun might shine,
  I joined his suit, gave over mine,
And sought Ione, to plead for him.

Lyrics of Lowly Life.

I found her in an eastern bower,
   Where all day long the am'rous sun
Lay by to woo a timid flower.
   This day his course was well-nigh run,
   But still with lingering art he spun
Gold fancies on the shadowed wall.
   The vines waved soft and green above,
   And there where one might tell his love,
I told my griefs — I told her all !

I told her all, and as she hearkened,
   A tear-drop fell upon her dress.
With grief her flushing brow was darkened ;
   One sob that she could not repress
   Betrayed the depths of her distress.
Upon her grief my sorrow fed,
   And I was bowed with unlived years,
   My heart swelled with a sea of tears,
The tears my manhood could not shed.

The world is Rome, and Fate is Nero,
   Disporting in the hour of doom.
God made us men ; times make the hero —
   But in that awful space of gloom

Lyrics of Lowly Life.

I gave no thought but sorrow's room.
All — all was dim within that bower,
    What time the sun divorced the day;
    And all the shadows, glooming gray,
Proclaimed the sadness of the hour.

She could not speak — no word was needed;
    Her look, half strength and half despair,
Told me I had not vainly pleaded,
    That she would not ignore my prayer.
    And so she turned and left me there,
And as she went, so passed my bliss;
    She loved me, I could not mistake —
    But for her own and my love's sake,
Her womanhood could rise to this!

My wounded heart fled swift to cover,
    And life at times seemed very drear.
My brother proved an ardent lover —
    What had so young a man to fear?
    He wed Ione within the year.

No shadow clouds her tranquil brow,
  Men speak her husband's name with pride,
  While she sits honored at his side —
She is — she must be happy now !

I doubt the course I took no longer,
  Since those I love seem satisfied.
The bond between them will grow stronger
  As they go forward side by side ;
  Then will my pains be justified.
Their joy is mine, and that is best —
  I am not totally bereft ;
  For I have still the mem'ry left —
Love stopped with me — a Royal Guest !

RELIGION.

I AM no priest of crooks nor creeds,
  For human wants and human needs
Are more to me than prophets' deeds ;
And human tears and human cares
Affect me more than human prayers.

Lyrics of Lowly Life.

Go, cease your wail, lugubrious saint!
You fret high Heaven with your plaint.
Is this the " Christian's joy " you paint?
Is this the Christian's boasted bliss?
Avails your faith no more than this?

Take up your arms, come out with me,
Let Heav'n alone; humanity
Needs more and Heaven less from thee.
With pity for mankind look 'round;
Help them to rise — and Heaven is found.

DEACON JONES' GRIEVANCE.

I 'VE been watchin' of 'em, parson,
   An' I 'm sorry fur to say
'At my mind is not contented
   With the loose an' keerless way
'At the young folks treat the music;
   'T ain't the proper sort o' choir.
Then I don't believe in Christuns
   A-singin' hymns for hire.

Lyrics of Lowly Life.

But I never would 'a' murmured
   An' the matter might 'a' gone
Ef it was n't fur the antics
   'At I 've seen 'em kerry on ;
So I thought it was my dooty
   Fur to come to you an' ask
Ef you would n't sort o' gently
   Take them singin' folks to task.

Fust, the music they 've be'n singin'
   Will disgrace us mighty soon ;
It 's a cross between a opry
   An' a ol' cotillion tune.
With its dashes an' its quavers
   An' its hifalutin style —
Why, it sets my head to swimmin'
   When I 'm comin' down the aisle.

Now it might be almost decent
   Ef it was n't fur the way
'At they git up there an' sing it,
   Hey dum diddle, loud and gay.

Lyrics of Lowly Life.

Why, it shames the name o' sacred
   In its brazen worldliness,
An' they 've even got " Ol' Hundred "
   In a bold, new-fangled dress.

You 'll excuse me, Mr. Parson,
   Ef I seem a little sore ;
But I 've sung the songs of Isr'el
   For threescore years an' more,
An' it sort o' hurts my feelin's
   Fur to see 'em put away
Fur these harum-scarum ditties
   'At is capturin' the day.

There 's anuther little happ'nin'
   'At I 'll mention while I 'm here,
Jes' to show 'at my objections
   All is offered sound and clear.
It was one day they was singin'
   An' was doin' well enough —
Singin' good as people could sing
   Sich an awful mess o' stuff —

Lyrics of Lowly Life.

When the choir give a holler,
   An' the organ give a groan,
An' they left one weak-voiced feller
   A-singin' there alone !
But he stuck right to the music,
   Tho' 't was tryin' as could be ;
An' when I tried to help him,
   Why, the hull church scowled at me.

You say that 's so-low singin',
   Well, I pray the Lord that I
Growed up when folks was willin'
   To sing their hymns so high.
Why, we never had sich doin's
   In the good ol' Bethel days,
When the folks was all contented
   With the simple songs of praise.

Now I may have spoke too open,
   But 't was too hard to keep still,
An' I hope you 'll tell the singers
   'At I bear 'em no ill-will.

Lyrics of Lowly Life.

'At they all may git to glory
  Is my wish an' my desire,
But they 'll need some extry trainin'
  'Fore they jine the heavenly choir.

ALICE.

KNOW you, winds that blow your course
    Down the verdant valleys,
That somewhere you must, perforce,
  Kiss the brow of Alice?
When her gentle face you find,
Kiss it softly, naughty wind.

Roses waving fair and sweet
  Thro' the garden alleys,
Grow into a glory meet
  For the eye of Alice ;
Let the wind your offering bear
Of sweet perfume, faint and rare.

Lyrics of Lowly Life.

Lily holding crystal dew
   In your pure white chalice,
Nature kind hath fashioned you
   Like the soul of Alice ;
It of purest white is wrought,
Filled with gems of crystal thought.

AFTER THE QUARREL.

SO we, who 've supped the self-same cup,
   To-night must lay our friendship by ;
Your wrath has burned your judgment up,
   Hot breath has blown the ashes high.
You say that you are wronged — ah, well,
   I count that friendship poor, at best
A bauble, a mere bagatelle,
   That cannot stand so slight a test.

I fain would still have been your friend,
   And talked and laughed and loved with you ;
But since it must, why, let it end ;
   The false but dies, 't is not the true.

Lyrics of Lowly Life.

So we are favored, you and I,
　　Who only want the living truth.
It was not good to nurse the lie ;
　　'T is well it died in harmless youth.

I go from you to-night to sleep.
　　Why, what's the odds? why should I grieve?
I have no fund of tears to weep
　　For happenings that undeceive.
The days shall come, the days shall go
　　Just as they came and went before.
The sun shall shine, the streams shall flow
　　Though you and I are friends no more.

And in the volume of my years,
　　Where all my thoughts and acts shall be,
The page whereon your name appears
　　Shall be forever sealed to me.
Not that I hate you over-much,
　　'T is less of hate than love defied ;
Howe'er, our hands no more shall touch,
　　We 'll go our ways, the world is wide.

BEYOND THE YEARS.

I.

BEYOND the years the answer lies,
 Beyond where brood the grieving skies
 And Night drops tears.
Where Faith rod-chastened smiles to rise
 And doff its fears,
And carping Sorrow pines and dies —
 Beyond the years.

II.

Beyond the years the prayer for rest
Shall beat no more within the breast;
 The darkness clears,
And Morn perched on the mountain's crest
 Her form uprears —
The day that is to come is best,
 Beyond the years.

Lyrics of Lowly Life.

III.

Beyond the years the soul shall find
That endless peace for which it pined,
    For light appears,
And to the eyes that still were blind
    With blood and tears,
Their sight shall come all unconfined
    Beyond the years.

AFTER A VISIT.

I BE'N down in ole Kentucky
    Fur a week er two, an' say,
'T wuz ez hard ez breakin' oxen
    Fur to tear myse'f away.
Allus argerin' 'bout fren'ship
    An' yer hospitality —
Y' ain't no right to talk about it
    Tell you be'n down there to see.

See jest how they give you welcom
    To the best that 's in the land,

Lyrics of Lowly Life.

Feel the sort o' grip they give you
   When they take you by the hand.
Hear 'em say, " We 're glad to have you,
   Better stay a week er two ; "
An' the way they treat you makes you
   Feel that ev'ry word is true.

Feed you tell you hear the buttons
   Crackin' on yore Sunday vest ;
Haul you roun' to see the wonders
   Tell you have to cry for rest.
Drink yer health an' pet an' praise you
   Tell you git to feel ez great
Ez the Sheriff o' the county
   Er the Gov'ner o' the State.

Wife, she sez I must be crazy
   'Cause I go on so, an' Nelse
He 'lows, " Goodness gracious ! daddy,
   Cain't you talk about nuthin' else ? "
Well, pleg-gone it, I 'm jes' tickled,
   Bein' tickled ain't no sin ;
I be'n down in ole Kentucky,
   An' I want o' go ag'in.

Lyrics of Lowly Life.

CURTAIN.

VILLAIN shows his indiscretion,
  Villain's partner makes confession.
Juvenile, with golden tresses,
Finds her pa and dons long dresses.
Scapegrace comes home money-laden,
Hero comforts tearful maiden,
Soubrette marries loyal chappie,
Villain skips, and all are happy.

THE SPELLIN'-BEE.

I NEVER shall furgit that night when father
    hitched up Dobbin,
An' all us youngsters clambered in an' down the
    road went bobbin'
To school where we was kep' at work in every
    kind o' weather,
But where that night a spellin'-bee was callin' us
    together.

93

Lyrics of Lowly Life.

'T was one o' Heaven's banner nights, the stars
    was all a glitter,
The moon was shinin' like the hand o' God had
    jest then lit her.
The ground was white with spotless snow, the
    blast was sort o' stingin';
But underneath our round-abouts, you bet our
    hearts was singin'.
That spellin'-bee had be'n the talk o' many a
    precious moment,
The youngsters all was wild to see jes' what the
    precious show meant,
An' we whose years was in their teens was little
    less desirous
O' gittin' to the meetin' so 's our sweethearts
    could admire us.
So on we went so anxious fur to satisfy our
    mission
That father had to box our ears, to smother our
    ambition.
But boxin' ears was too short work to hinder
    our arrivin',

94

He jest turned roun' an' smacked us all, an' kep'
    right on a-drivin'.
Well, soon the schoolhouse hove in sight, the
    winders beamin' brightly;
The sound o' talkin' reached our ears, and voices
    laffin' lightly.
It puffed us up so full an' big 'at I 'll jest bet a
    dollar,
There wa'n't a feller there but felt the strain
    upon his collar.
So down we jumped an' in we went ez sprightly
    ez you make 'em,
But somethin' grabbed us by the knees an'
    straight began to shake 'em.
Fur once within that lighted room, our feelin's
    took a canter,
An' scurried to the zero mark ez quick ez Tam
    O'Shanter.
'Cause there was crowds o' people there, both
    sexes an' all stations;
It looked like all the town had come an' brought
    all their relations.

Lyrics of Lowly Life.

The first I saw was Nettie Gray, I thought that
    girl was dearer
'N' gold; an' when I got a chance, you bet I
    aidged up near her.
An' Farmer Dobbs's girl was there, the one 'at
    Jim was sweet on,
An' Cyrus Jones an' Mandy Smith an' Faith an'
    Patience Deaton.
Then Parson Brown an' Lawyer Jones were
    present — all attention,
An' piles on piles of other folks too numerous
    to mention.
The master rose an' briefly said : "Good friends,
    dear brother Crawford,
To spur the pupils' minds along, a little prize
    has offered.
To him who spells the best to-night — or 't may
    be 'her' — no tellin' —
He offers ez a jest reward, this precious work on
    spellin'."
A little blue-backed spellin'-book with fancy
    scarlet trimmin' ;

Lyrics of Lowly Life.

We boys devoured it with our eyes — so did the
girls an' women.
He held it up where all could see, then on the
table set it,
An' ev'ry speller in the house felt mortal bound
to get it.
At his command we fell in line, prepared to do
our dooty,
Outspell the rest an' set 'em down, an' carry
home the booty.
'T was then the merry times began, the blunders,
an' the laffin',
The nudges an' the nods an' winks an' stale
good-natured chaffin'.
Ole Uncle Hiram Dane was there, the clostest
man a-livin',
Whose only bugbear seemed to be the dreadful
fear o' givin'.
His beard was long, his hair uncut, his clothes
all bare an' dingy ;
It was n't 'cause the man was pore, but jest so
mortal stingy.

An' there he sot by Sally Riggs a-smilin' an'
    a-smirkin',
An' all his childern lef' to home a diggin' an'
    a-workin'.
A widower he was, an' Sal was thinkin' 'at she 'd
    wing him ;
I reckon he was wond'rin' what them rings o'
    hern would bring him.
An' when the spellin'-test commenced, he up
    an' took his station,
A-spellin' with the best o' them to beat the very
    nation.
An' when he 'd spell some youngster down, he 'd
    turn to look at Sally,
An' say : " The teachin' nowadays can't be o'
    no great vally."
But true enough the adage says, " Pride walks
    in slipp'ry places,"
Fur soon a thing occurred that put a smile on
    all our faces.
The laffter jest kep' ripplin' 'roun' an' teacher
    could n't quell it,

Fur when he give out " charity " ole Hiram
    could n't spell it.

But laffin' 's ketchin' an' it throwed some others
    off their bases,

An' folks 'u'd miss the very word that seemed
    to fit their cases.

Why, fickle little Jessie Lee come near the
    house upsettin'

By puttin' in a double " kay " to spell the word
    " coquettin'."

An' when it come to Cyrus Jones, it tickled me
    all over —

Him settin' up to Mandy Smith an' got sot
    down on " lover."

But Lawyer Jones of all gone men did shorely
    look the gonest,

When he found out that he 'd furgot to put the
    " h " in " honest."

An' Parson Brown, whose sermons were too long
    fur toleration,

Caused lots o' smiles by missin' when they give
    out " condensation."

Lyrics of Lowly Life.

So one by one they giv' it up — the big words
  kep' a-landin',
Till me an' Nettie Gray was left, the only ones
  a-standin',
An' then my inward strife began — I guess my
  mind was petty —
I did so want that spellin'-book ; but then to
  spell down Nettie
Jest sort o' went ag'in my grain — I somehow
  could n't do it,
An' when I git a notion fixed, I 'm great on
  stickin' to it.
So when they giv' the next word out — I had n't
  orter tell it,
But then 't was all fur Nettie's sake — I missed
  so 's she could spell it.
She spelt the word, then looked at me so lovin'-
  like an' mello',
I tell you 't sent a hunderd pins a-shootin'
  through a fello'.
O' course I had to stand the jokes an' chaffin'
  of the fello's,

But when they handed her the book I vow I
    was n't jealous.

We sung a hymn, an' Parson Brown dismissed us
    like he orter,

Fur, la ! he 'd learned a thing er two an' made
    his blessin' shorter.

'T was late an' cold when we got out, but Nettie
    liked cold weather,

An' so did I, so we agreed we 'd jest walk home
    together.

We both wuz silent, fur of words we nuther had
    a surplus,

'Till she spoke out quite sudden like, " You
    missed that word on purpose."

Well, I declare it frightened me ; at first I tried
    denyin',

But Nettie, she jest smiled an' smiled, she
    knowed that I was lyin'.

Sez she : " That book is yourn by right ; " sez
    I : " It never could be —

I — I — you — ah —— " an' there I stuck, an'
    well she understood me.

So we agreed that later on when age had giv'
    us tether,
We 'd jine our lots an' settle down to own that
    book together.

KEEP A–PLUGGIN' AWAY.

I 'VE a humble little motto
    That is homely, though it 's true, —
  Keep a-pluggin' away.
It 's a thing when I 've an object
That I always try to do, —
  Keep a-pluggin' away.
When you 've rising storms to quell,
When opposing waters swell,
It will never fail to tell, —
  Keep a-pluggin' away.

If the hills are high before
And the paths are hard to climb,
  Keep a-pluggin' away.

Lyrics of Lowly Life.

And remember that successes
Come to him who bides his time, —
   Keep a-pluggin' away.
From the greatest to the least,
None are from the rule released.
Be thou toiler, poet, priest,
   Keep a-pluggin' away.

Delve away beneath the surface,
There is treasure farther down, —
   Keep a-pluggin' away.
Let the rain come down in torrents,
Let the threat'ning heavens frown,
   Keep a-pluggin' away.
When the clouds have rolled away,
There will come a brighter day
All your labor to repay, —
   Keep a-pluggin' away.

There 'll be lots of sneers to swallow,
There 'll be lots of pain to bear, —
   Keep a-pluggin' away.

Lyrics of Lowly Life.

If you 've got your eye on heaven,
Some bright day you 'll wake up there,
  Keep a-pluggin' away.
Perseverance still is king;
Time its sure reward will bring;
Work and wait unwearying, —
  Keep a-pluggin' away.

NIGHT OF LOVE.

THE moon has left the sky, love,
  The stars are hiding now,
And frowning on the world, love,
  Night bares her sable brow.
The snow is on the ground, love,
  And cold and keen the air is.
I 'm singing here to you, love;
  You 're dreaming there in Paris.

But this is Nature's law, love,
  Though just it may not seem,
That men should wake to sing, love,
  While maidens sleep and dream.

Lyrics of Lowly Life.

Them care may not molest, love,
  Nor stir them from their slumbers,
Though midnight find the swain, love,
  Still halting o'er his numbers.

I watch the rosy dawn, love,
  Come stealing up the east,
While all things round rejoice, love,
  That Night her reign has ceased.
The lark will soon be heard, love,
  And on his way be winging ;
When Nature's poets wake, love,
  Why should a man be singing ?

COLUMBIAN ODE.

I.

FOUR hundred years ago a tangled waste
  Lay sleeping on the west Atlantic's side ;
Their devious ways the Old World's millions
      traced
  Content, and loved, and labored, dared and
      died,

Lyrics of Lowly Life.

While students still believed the charts they
    conned,
  And revelled in their thriftless ignorance,
Nor dreamed of other lands that lay beyond
  Old Ocean's dense, indefinite expanse.

II.

But deep within her heart old Nature knew
  That she had once arrayed, at Earth's behest,
Another offspring, fine and fair to view, —
  The chosen suckling of the mother's breast.
The child was wrapped in vestments soft and
    fine,
  Each fold a work of Nature's matchless art;
The mother looked on it with love divine,
  And strained the loved one closely to her
    heart.
And there it lay, and with the warmth grew
    strong
  And hearty, by the salt sea breezes fanned,
Till Time with mellowing touches passed along,
  And changed the infant to a mighty land.

Lyrics of Lowly Life.

III.

BUT men knew naught of this, till there arose
  That mighty mariner, the Genoese,
Who dared to try, in spite of fears and foes,
  The unknown fortunes of unsounded seas.
O noblest of Italia's sons, thy bark
  Went not alone into that shrouding night!
O dauntless darer of the rayless dark,
  The world sailed with thee to eternal light!
The deer-haunts that with game were crowded
        then
  To-day are tilled and cultivated lands;
The schoolhouse tow'rs where Bruin had his
        den,
    And where the wigwam stood the chapel
        stands;
The place that nurtured men of savage mien
  Now teems with men of Nature's noblest
        types;
Where moved the forest-foliage banner green,
  Now flutters in the breeze the stars and
        stripes!

Lyrics of Lowly Life.

A BORDER BALLAD.

OH, I have n't got long to live, for we all
  Die soon, e'en those who live longest;
And the poorest and weakest are taking their
    chance
  Along with the richest and strongest.
So it 's heigho for a glass and a song,
  And a bright eye over the table,
And a dog for the hunt when the game is flush,
  And the pick of a gentleman's stable.

There is Dimmock o' Dune, he was here yester-
    night,
  But he 's rotting to-day on Glen Arragh;
'T was the hand o' MacPherson that gave him
    the blow,
  And the vultures shall feast on his marrow.
But it 's heigho for a brave old song
  And a glass while we are able;
Here 's a health to death and another cup
  To the bright eye over the table.

Lyrics of Lowly Life.

I can show a broad back and a jolly deep chest,
  But who argues now on appearance?
A blow or a thrust or a stumble at best
  May send me to-day to my clearance.
Then it's heigho for the things I love,
  My mother 'll be soon wearing sable,
But give me my horse and my dog and my
      glass,
  And a bright eye over the table.

AN EASY-GOIN' FELLER.

THER' ain't no use in all this strife,
    An' hurryin', pell-mell, right thro' life.
I don't believe in goin' too fast
To see what kind o' road you 've passed.
It ain't no mortal kind o' good,
'N' I would n't hurry ef I could.
I like to jest go joggin' 'long,
To limber up my soul with song;
To stop awhile 'n' chat the men,
'N' drink some cider now an' then.

Do' want no boss a-standin' by
To see me work ; I allus try
To do my dooty right straight up,
An' earn what fills my plate an' cup.
An' ez fur boss, I 'll be my own,
I like to jest be let alone,
To plough my strip an' tend my bees,
An' do jest like I doggoned please.
My head 's all right, an' my heart 's meller,
But I 'm a easy-goin' feller.

A NEGRO LOVE SONG.

SEEN my lady home las' night,
    Jump back, honey, jump back.
Hel' huh han' an' sque'z it tight,
    Jump back, honey, jump back.
Hyeahd huh sigh a little sigh,
Seen a light gleam f'om huh eye,
An' a smile go flittin' by —
    Jump back, honey, jump back.

Lyrics of Lowly Life.

Hyeahd de win' blow thoo de pine,
  Jump back, honey, jump back.
Mockin'-bird was singin' fine,
  Jump back, honey, jump back.
An' my hea't was beatin' so,
When I reached my lady's do',
Dat I could n't ba' to go —
  Jump back, honey, jump back.

Put my ahm aroun' huh wais',
  Jump back, honey, jump back.
Raised huh lips an' took a tase,
  Jump back, honey, jump back.
Love me, honey, love me true?
Love me well ez I love you?
An' she answe'd, " 'Cose I do " —
  Jump back, honey, jump back.

THE DILETTANTE: A MODERN TYPE.

HE scribbles some in prose and verse,
    And now and then he prints it;
He paints a little, — gathers some
    Of Nature's gold and mints it.

He plays a little, sings a song,
    Acts tragic rôles, or funny;
He does, because his love is strong,
    But not, oh, not for money!

He studies almost everything
    From social art to science;
A thirsty mind, a flowing spring,
    Demand and swift compliance.

He looms above the sordid crowd —
    At least through friendly lenses;
While his mamma looks pleased and proud,
    And kindly pays expenses.

Lyrics of Lowly Life.

BY THE STREAM.

BY the stream I dream in calm delight, and
    watch as in a glass,
How the clouds like crowds of snowy-hued and
    white-robed maidens pass,
And the water into ripples breaks and sparkles
    as it spreads,
Like a host of armored knights with silver
    helmets on their heads.
And I deem the stream an emblem fit of human
    life may go,
For I find a mind may sparkle much and yet
    but shallows show,
And a soul may glow with myriad lights and
    wondrous mysteries,
When it only lies a dormant thing and mirrors
    what it sees.

113

THE COLORED SOLDIERS.

IF the muse were mine to tempt it
  And my feeble voice were strong,
If my tongue were trained to measures,
  I would sing a stirring song.
I would sing a song heroic
  Of those noble sons of Ham,
Of the gallant colored soldiers
  Who fought for Uncle Sam !

In the early days you scorned them,
  And with many a flip and flout
Said " These battles are the white man's,
  And the whites will fight them out."
Up the hills you fought and faltered,
  In the vales you strove and bled,
While your ears still heard the thunder
  Of the foes' advancing tread.

Lyrics of Lowly Life.

Then distress fell on the nation,
    And the flag was drooping low;
Should the dust pollute your banner?
    No! the nation shouted, No!
So when War, in savage triumph,
    Spread abroad his funeral pall—
Then you called the colored soldiers,
    And they answered to your call.

And like hounds unleashed and eager
    For the life blood of the prey,
Sprung they forth and bore them bravely
    In the thickest of the fray.
And where'er the fight was hottest,
    Where the bullets fastest fell,
There they pressed unblanched and fearless
    At the very mouth of hell.

Ah, they rallied to the standard
    To uphold it by their might;
None were stronger in the labors,
    None were braver in the fight.

Lyrics of Lowly Life.

From the blazing breach of Wagner
   To the plains of Olustee,
They were foremost in the fight
   Of the battles of the free.

And at Pillow !   God have mercy
   On the deeds committed there,
And the souls of those poor victims
   Sent to Thee without a prayer.
Let the fulness of Thy pity
   O'er the hot wrought spirits sway
Of the gallant colored soldiers
   Who fell fighting on that day !

Yes, the Blacks enjoy their freedom,
   And they won it dearly, too ;
For the life blood of their thousands
   Did the southern fields bedew.
In the darkness of their bondage,
   In the depths of slavery's night,
Their muskets flashed the dawning,
   And they fought their way to light.

Lyrics of Lowly Life.

They were comrades then and brothers,
  Are they more or less to-day?
They were good to stop a bullet
  And to front the fearful fray.
They were citizens and soldiers,
  When rebellion raised its head;
And the traits that made them worthy,—
  Ah! those virtues are not dead.

They have shared your nightly vigils,
  They have shared your daily toil;
And their blood with yours commingling
  Has enriched the Southern soil.
They have slept and marched and suffered
  'Neath the same dark skies as you,
They have met as fierce a foeman,
  And have been as brave and true.

And their deeds shall find a record
  In the registry of Fame;
For their blood has cleansed completely
  Every blot of Slavery's shame.

Lyrics of Lowly Life.

So all honor and all glory
　　To those noble sons of Ham —
The gallant colored soldiers
　　Who fought for Uncle Sam !

NATURE AND ART.

TO MY FRIEND CHARLES BOOTH NETTLETON.

I.

THE young queen Nature, ever sweet and
　　fair,
　　Once on a time fell upon evil days.
　　From hearing oft herself discussed with
　　　　praise,
There grew within her heart the longing rare
To see herself; and every passing air
　　The warm desiré fanned into lusty blaze.
　　Full oft she sought this end by devious
　　　　ways,
But sought in vain, so fell she in despair.

118

Lyrics of Lowly Life.

For none within her train nor by her side
    Could solve the task or give the envied
        boon.
    So day and night, beneath the sun and
        moon,
She wandered to and fro unsatisfied,
    Till Art came by, a blithe inventive elf,
    And made a glass wherein she saw herself.

II.

Enrapt, the queen gazed on her glorious self,
    Then trembling with the thrill of sudden
        thought,
    Commanded that the skilful wight be brought
That she might dower him with lands and pelf.
Then out upon the silent sea-lapt shelf
    And up the hills and on the downs they
        sought
    Him who so well and wondrously had
        wrought ;
And with much search found and brought home
        the elf.
    But he put by all gifts with sad replies,

And from his lips these words flowed forth like
    wine :
   " O queen, I want no gift but thee," he said.
She heard and looked on him with love-lit
    eyes,
Gave him her hand, low murmuring, " I am
    thine,"
   And at the morrow's dawning they were wed.

AFTER WHILE.

A POEM OF FAITH.

I THINK that though the clouds be dark,
   That though the waves dash o'er the bark,
Yet after while the light will come,
And in calm waters safe at home
    The bark will anchor.
Weep not, my sad-eyed, gray-robed maid,
Because your fairest blossoms fade,
That sorrow still o'erruns your cup,
And even though you root them up,
    The weeds grow ranker.

120

Lyrics of Lowly Life.

For after while your tears shall cease,
And sorrow shall give way to peace;
The flowers shall bloom, the weeds shall die,
And in that faith seen, by and by
    Thy woes shall perish.
Smile at old Fortune's adverse tide,
Smile when the scoffers sneer and chide.
Oh, not for you the gems that pale,
And not for you the flowers that fail;
    Let this thought cherish:

That after while the clouds will part,
And then with joy the waiting heart
Shall feel the light come stealing in,
That drives away the cloud of sin
    And breaks its power.
And you shall burst your chrysalis,
And wing away to realms of bliss,
Untrammelled, pure, divinely free,
Above all earth's anxiety
    From that same hour.

THE OL' TUNES.

YOU kin talk about yer anthems
    An' yer arias an' sich,
An' yer modern choir-singin'
    That you think so awful rich;
But you orter heerd us youngsters
    In the times now far away,
A-singin' o' the ol' tunes
    In the ol'-fashioned way.

There was some of us sung treble
    An' a few of us growled bass,
An' the tide o' song flowed smoothly
    With its 'comp'niment o' grace;
There was spirit in that music,
    An' a kind o' solemn sway,
A-singin' o' the ol' tunes
    In the ol'-fashioned way.

122

Lyrics of Lowly Life.

I remember oft o' standin'
   In my homespun pantaloons —
On my face the bronze an' freckles
   O' the suns o' youthful Junes —
Thinkin' that no mortal minstrel
   Ever chanted sich a lay
As the ol' tunes we was singin'
   In the ol'-fashioned way.

The boys 'ud always lead us,
   An' the girls 'ud all chime in,
Till the sweetness o' the singin'
   Robbed the list'nin' soul o' sin ;
An' I used to tell the parson
   'T was as good to sing as pray,
When the people sung the ol' tunes
   In the ol'-fashioned way.

How I long ag'in to hear 'em
   Pourin' forth from soul to soul,
With the treble high an' meller,
   An' the bass's mighty roll ;

123

Lyrics of Lowly Life.

But the times is very diff'rent,
   An' the music heerd to-day
Ain't the singin' o' the ol' tunes
   In the ol'-fashioned way.

Little screechin' by a woman,
   Little squawkin' by a man,
Then the organ's twiddle-twaddle,
   Jest the empty space to span, —
An' ef you should even think it,
   'T is n't proper fur to say
That you want to hear the ol' tunes
   In the ol'-fashioned way.

But I think that some bright mornin',
   When the toils of life air o'er,
An' the sun o' heaven arisin'
   Glads with light the happy shore,
I shall hear the angel chorus,
   In the realms of endless day,
A-singin' o' the ol' tunes
   In the ol'-fashioned way.

MELANCHOLIA.

SILENTLY without my window,
   Tapping gently at the pane,
   Falls the rain.
Through the trees sighs the breeze
   Like a soul in pain.
Here alone I sit and weep ;
Thought hath banished sleep.

Wearily I sit and listen
   To the water's ceaseless drip.
   To my lip
Fate turns up the bitter cup,
   Forcing me to sip ;
'T is a bitter, bitter drink,
Thus I sit and think, —

Lyrics of Lowly Life.

Thinking things unknown and awful,
   Thoughts on wild, uncanny themes,
   Waking dreams.
Spectres dark, corpses stark,
   Show the gaping séams
Whence the cold and cruel knife
Stole away their life.

Bloodshot eyes all strained and staring,
   Gazing ghastly into mine ;
   Blood like wine
On the brow — clotted now —
   Shows death's dreadful sign.
Lonely vigil still I keep ;
Would that I might sleep !

Still, oh, still, my brain is whirling !
   Still runs on my stream of thought ;
   I am caught
In the net fate hath set.
   Mind and soul are brought
To destruction's very brink ;
Yet I can but think !

Lyrics of Lowly Life.

Eyes that look into the future, —
  Peeping forth from out my mind,
  They will find
Some new weight, soon or late,
  On my soul to bind,
Crushing all its courage out, —
Heavier than doubt.

Dawn, the Eastern monarch's daughter,
  Rising from her dewy bed,
  Lays her head
'Gainst the clouds' sombre shrouds
  Now half fringed with red.
O'er the land she 'gins to peep ;
Come, O gentle Sleep !

Hark ! the morning cock is crowing ;
  Dreams, like ghosts, must hie away ;
  'T is the day.
Rosy morn now is born ;
  Dark thoughts may not stay.
Day my brain from foes will keep ;
Now, my soul, I sleep.

THE WOOING.

A YOUTH went faring up and down,
        Alack and well-a-day.
He fared him to the market town,
        Alack and well-a-day.
And there he met a maiden fair,
With hazel eyes and auburn hair;
His heart went from him then and there,
        Alack and well-a-day.

She posies sold right merrily,
        Alack and well-a-day;
But not a flower was fair as she,
        Alack and well-a-day.
He bought a rose and sighed a sigh,
" Ah, dearest maiden, would that I
Might dare the seller too to buy ! "
        Alack and well-a-day.

Lyrics of Lowly Life.

She tossed her head, the coy coquette,
  Alack and well-a-day.
" I 'm not, sir, in the market yet,"
  Alack and well-a-day.
" Your love must cool upon a shelf;
Tho' much I sell for gold and pelf,
I 'm yet too young to sell myself,"
  Alack and well-a-day.

The youth was filled with sorrow sore,
  Alack and well-a-day ;
And looked he at the maid once more,
  Alack and well-a-day.
Then loud he cried, " Fair maiden, if
Too young to sell, now as I live,
You 're not too young yourself to give,"
  Alack and well-a-day.

The little maid cast down her eyes,
  Alack and well-a-day,
And many a flush began to rise,
  Alack and well-a-day.

129

Lyrics of Lowly Life.

"Why, since you are so bold," she said,
"I doubt not you are highly bred,
So take me!" and the twain were wed,
　　Alack and well-a-day.

MERRY AUTUMN.

IT's all a farce, — these tales they tell
　　About the breezes sighing,
And moans astir o'er field and dell,
　　Because the year is dying.

Such principles are most absurd, —
　　I care not who first taught 'em;
There's nothing known to beast or bird
　　To make a solemn autumn.

In solemn times, when grief holds sway
　　With countenance distressing,
You'll note the more of black and gray
　　Will then be used in dressing.

130

Lyrics of Lowly Life.

Now purple tints are all around;
  The sky is blue and mellow;
And e'en the grasses turn the ground
  From modest green to yellow.

The seed burrs all with laughter crack
  On featherweed and jimson;
And leaves that should be dressed in black
  Are all decked out in crimson.

A butterfly goes winging by;
  A singing bird comes after;
And Nature, all from earth to sky,
  Is bubbling o'er with laughter.

The ripples wimple on the rills,
  Like sparkling little lasses;
The sunlight runs along the hills,
  And laughs among the grasses.

The earth is just so full of fun
  It really can't contain it;
And streams of mirth so freely run
  The heavens seem to rain it.

Lyrics of Lowly Life.

Don't talk to me of solemn days
   In autumn's time of splendor,
Because the sun shows fewer rays,
   And these grow slant and slender.

Why, it 's the climax of the year, —
   The highest time of living ! —
Till naturally its bursting cheer
   Just melts into thanksgiving.

WHEN DE CO'N PONE 'S HOT.

DEY is times in life when Nature
   Seems to slip a cog an' go,
Jes' a-rattlin' down creation,
   Lak an ocean's overflow ;
When de worl' jes' stahts a-spinnin'
   Lak a picaninny's top,
An' yo' cup o' joy is brimmin'
   'Twell it seems about to slop,

Lyrics of Lowly Life.

An' you feel jes' lak a racah,
   Dat is trainin' fu' to trot —
When yo' mammy says de blessin'
   An' de co'n pone 's hot.

When you set down at de table,
   Kin' o' weary lak an' sad,
An' you 'se jes' a little tiahed
   An' purhaps a little mad ;
How yo' gloom tu'ns into gladness,
   How yo' joy drives out de doubt
When de oven do' is opened,
   An' de smell comes po'in' out ;
Why, de 'lectric light o' Heaven
   Seems to settle on de spot,
When yo' mammy says de blessin'
   An' de co'n pone 's hot.

When de cabbage pot is steamin'
   An' de bacon good an' fat,
When de chittlins is a-sputter'n'
   So 's to show you whah dey 's at ;

Lyrics of Lowly Life.

Tek away yo' sody biscuit,
  Tek away yo' cake an' pie,
Fu' de glory time is comin',
  An' it 's 'proachin' mighty nigh,
An' you want to jump an' hollah,
  Dough you know you 'd bettah not,
When yo' mammy says de blessin',
  An' de co'n pone 's hot.

I have hyeahd o' lots o' sermons,
  An' I 've hyeahd o' lots o' prayers,
An' I 've listened to some singin'
  Dat has tuck me up de stairs
Of de Glory-Lan' an' set me
  Jes' below de Mahstah's th'one,
An' have lef' my hea't a-singin'
  In a happy aftah tone ;
But dem wu'ds so sweetly murmured
  Seem to tech de softes' spot,
When my mammy says de blessin',
  An' de co'n pone 's hot.

Lyrics of Lowly Life.

BALLAD.

I KNOW my love is true,
    And oh the day is fair.
The sky is clear and blue,
The flowers are rich of hue,
    The air I breathe is rare,
    I have no grief or care;
For my own love is true,
    And oh the day is fair.

My love is false I find,
    And oh the day is dark.
Blows sadly down the wind,
While sorrow holds my mind;
    I do not hear the lark,
    For quenched is life's dear spark, —
My love is false I find,
    And oh the day is dark!

For love doth make the day
    Or dark or doubly bright;
Her beams along the way
Dispel the gloom and gray.

Lyrics of Lowly Life.

She lives and all is bright,
She dies and life is night.
For love doth make the day,
Or dark or doubly bright.

THE CHANGE HAS COME.

THE change has come, and Helen sleeps —
    Not sleeps; but wakes to greater deeps
Of wisdom, glory, truth, and light,
Than ever blessed her seeking sight,
In this low, long, lethargic night,
        Worn out with strife
        Which men call life.

The change has come, and who would say
"I would it were not come to-day"?
    What were the respite till to-morrow?
    Postponement of a certain sorrow,
    From which each passing day would borrow!
        Let grief be dumb,
        The change has come.

Lyrics of Lowly Life.

COMPARISON.

THE sky of brightest gray seems dark
  To one whose sky was ever white.
To one who never knew a spark,
 Thro' all his life, of love or light,
 The grayest cloud seems over-bright.

The robin sounds a beggar's note
 Where one the nightingale has heard,
But he for whom no silver throat
 Its liquid music ever stirred,
 Deems robin still the sweetest bird.

A CORN–SONG.

ON the wide veranda white,
  In the purple failing light,
Sits the master while the sun is lowly burning;
And his dreamy thoughts are drowned
In the softly flowing sound
Of the corn-songs of the field-hands slow
  returning.

Lyrics of Lowly Life.

> Oh, we hoe de co'n
> Since de ehly mo'n;
> Now de sinkin' sun
> Says de day is done.

O'er the fields with heavy tread,
Light of heart and high of head,
Though the halting steps be labored, slow, and
    weary;
Still the spirits brave and strong
Find a comforter in song,
And their corn-song rises ever loud and cheery.

> Oh, we hoe de co'n
> Since de ehly mo'n;
> Now de sinkin' sun
> Says de day is done.

To the master in his seat,
Comes the burden, full and sweet,
Of the mellow minor music growing clearer,
As the toilers raise the hymn,
Thro' the silence dusk and dim,
To the cabin's restful shelter drawing nearer.

Lyrics of Lowly Life.

> Oh, we hoe de co'n
> Since de ehly mo'n;
> Now de sinkin' sun
> Says de day is done.

And a tear is in the eye
Of the master sitting by,
As he listens to the echoes low-replying
To the music's fading calls
As it faints away and falls
Into silence, deep within the cabin dying.

> Oh, we hoe de co'n
> Since de ehly mo'n;
> Now de sinkin' sun
> Says de day is done.

DISCOVERED.

SEEN you down at chu'ch las' night,
    Nevah min', Miss Lucy.
What I mean? oh, dat 's all right,
    Nevah min', Miss Lucy.

Lyrics of Lowly Life.

You was sma't ez sma't could be,
But you could n't hide f'om me.
Ain't I got two eyes to see!
   Nevah min', Miss Lucy.

Guess you thought you 's awful keen;
   Nevah min', Miss Lucy.
Evahthing you done, I seen;
   Nevah min', Miss Lucy.
Seen him tek yo' ahm jes' so,
When he got outside de do' —
Oh, I know dat man 's yo' beau!
   Nevah min', Miss Lucy.

Say now, honey, wha 'd he say? —
   Nevah min', Miss Lucy!
Keep yo' secrets — dat 's yo' way —
   Nevah min', Miss Lucy.
Won't tell me an' I 'm yo' pal —
I 'm gwine tell his othah gal, —
Know huh, too, huh name is Sal;
   Nevah min', Miss Lucy!

DISAPPOINTED.

AN old man planted and dug and tended,
   Toiling in joy from dew to dew;
The sun was kind, and the rain befriended;
   Fine grew his orchard and fair to view.
Then he said: "I will quiet my thrifty fears,
For here is fruit for my failing years."

But even then the storm-clouds gathered,
   Swallowing up the azure sky;
The sweeping winds into white foam lathered
   The placid breast of the bay, hard by;
Then the spirits that raged in the darkened air
Swept o'er his orchard and left it bare.

The old man stood in the rain, uncaring,
   Viewing the place the storm had swept;
And then with a cry from his soul despairing,
   He bowed him down to the earth and wept.
But a voice cried aloud from the driving rain;
"Arise, old man, and plant again!"

INVITATION TO LOVE.

COME when the nights are bright with
   stars
   Or when the moon is mellow;
Come when the sun his golden bars
   Drops on the hay-field yellow.
Come in the twilight soft and gray,
Come in the night or come in the day,
Come, O Love, whene'er you may,
   And you are welcome, welcome.

You are sweet, O Love, dear Love,
You are soft as the nesting dove.
Come to my heart and bring it rest
As the bird flies home to its welcome nest.

Come when my heart is full of grief
   Or when my heart is merry;
Come with the falling of the leaf
   Or with the redd'ning cherry.

142

Lyrics of Lowly Life.

Come when the year's first blossom blows,
Come when the summer gleams and glows,
Come with the winter's drifting snows,
    And you are welcome, welcome.

HE HAD HIS DREAM.

HE had his dream, and all through life,
    Worked up to it through toil and strife.
Afloat fore'er before his eyes,
It colored for him all his skies:
    The storm-cloud dark
    Above his bark,
The calm and listless vault of blue
Took on its hopeful hue,
It tinctured every passing beam —
    He had his dream.

He labored hard and failed at last,
His sails too weak to bear the blast,
The raging tempests tore away
And sent his beating bark astray.

143

But what cared he
For wind or sea !
He said, " The tempest will be short,
My bark will come to port."
He saw through every cloud a gleam —
He had his dream.

GOOD-NIGHT.

THE lark is silent in his nest,
   The breeze is sighing in its flight,
Sleep, Love, and peaceful be thy rest.
   Good-night, my love, good-night, good-night.

Sweet dreams attend thee in thy sleep,
   To soothe thy rest till morning's light,
And angels round thee vigil keep.
   Good-night, my love, good-night, good-night.

Sleep well, my love, on night's dark breast,
   And ease thy soul with slumber bright ;
Be joy but thine and I am blest.
   Good-night, my love, good-night, good-night.

Lyrics of Lowly Life.

A COQUETTE CONQUERED.

YES, my ha't 's ez ha'd ez stone —
  Go 'way, Sam, an' lemme 'lone.
No; I ain't gwine change my min' —
Ain't gwine ma'y you — nuffin' de kin'.

Phiny loves you true an' deah?
Go ma'y Phiny; whut I keer?
Oh, you need n't mou'n an' cry —
I don't keer how soon you die.

Got a present! Whut you got?
Somef'n fu' de pan er pot!
Huh! yo' sass do sholy beat —
Think I don't git 'nough to eat?

Whut 's dat un'neaf yo' coat?
Looks des lak a little shoat.
'T ain't no possum! Bless de Lamb!
Yes, it is, you rascal, Sam!

Gin it to me; whut you say?
Ain't you sma't now! Oh, go 'way!
Possum do look mighty nice,
But you ax too big a price.

Tell me, is you talkin' true,
Dat 's de gal's whut ma'ies you?
Come back, Sam; now whah 's you gwine?
Co'se you knows dat possum 's mine!

NORA: A SERENADE.

AH, Nora, my Nora, the light fades away,
    While Night like a spirit steals up o'er
      the hills;
The thrush from his tree where he chanted all
    day,
    No longer his music in ecstasy trills.
Then, Nora, be near me; thy presence doth
    cheer me,
    Thine eye hath a gleam that is truer than
      gold.

Lyrics of Lowly Life.

I cannot but love thee ; so do not reprove me,
   If the strength of my passion should make
      me too bold.

Nora, pride of my heart, —
   Rosy cheeks, cherry lips, sparkling with
      glee, —
Wake from thy slumbers, wherever thou art ;
   Wake from thy slumbers to me.

Ah, Nora, my Nora, there 's love in the air, —
   It stirs in the numbers that thrill in my brain ;
Oh, sweet, sweet is love with its mingling of
      care,
   Though joy travels only a step before pain.
Be roused from thy slumbers and list to my
      numbers ;
   My heart is poured out in this song unto
      thee.
Oh, be thou not cruel, thou treasure, thou
      jewel ;
   Turn thine ear to my pleading and hearken
      to me.

OCTOBER.

OCTOBER is the treasurer of the year,
And all the months pay bounty to her
store ;
The fields and orchards still their tribute bear,
And fill her brimming coffers more and more.
But she, with youthful lavishness,
Spends all her wealth in gaudy dress,
And decks herself in garments bold
Of scarlet, purple, red, and gold.

She heedeth not how swift the hours fly,
But smiles and sings her happy life along ;
She only sees above a shining sky ;
She only hears the breezes' voice in song.
Her garments trail the woodlands through,
And gather pearls of early dew
That sparkle, till the roguish Sun
Creeps up and steals them every one.

But what cares she that jewels should be lost,
   When all of Nature's bounteous wealth is
      hers?
Though princely fortunes may have been their
      cost,
   Not one regret her calm demeanor stirs.
Whole-hearted, happy, careless, free,
She lives her life out joyously,
   Nor cares when Frost stalks o'er her way
   And turns her auburn locks to gray.

A SUMMER'S NIGHT.

THE night is dewy as a maiden's mouth,
   The skies are bright as are a maiden's
      eyes,
   Soft as a maiden's breath the wind that flies
Up from the perfumed bosom of the South.

Lyrics of Lowly Life.

Like sentinels, the pines stand in the park;
  And hither hastening, like rakes that roam,
  With lamps to light their wayward footsteps
    home,
The fireflies come stagg'ring down the dark.

SHIPS THAT PASS IN THE NIGHT.

OUT in the sky the great dark clouds are
    massing;
  I look far out into the pregnant night,
Where I can hear a solemn booming gun
  And catch the gleaming of a random light,
That tells me that the ship I seek is passing,
    passing.

My tearful eyes my soul's deep hurt are
    glassing;
  For I would hail and check that ship of
    ships.

150

I stretch my hands imploring, cry aloud,
  My voice falls dead a foot from mine own
    lips,
And but its ghost doth reach that vessel, pass-
    ing, passing.

O Earth, O Sky, O Ocean, both surpassing,
  O heart of mine, O soul that dreads the
    dark !
Is there no hope for me ?   Is there no way
  That I may sight and check that speeding
    bark
Which out of sight and sound is passing,
    passing ?

THE DELINQUENT.

GOO'–BY, Jinks, I got to hump,
    Got to mek dis pony jump ;
See dat sun a-goin' down
'N' me a-foolin' hyeah in town !
    Git up, Suke — go long !

Lyrics of Lowly Life.

Guess Mirandy 'll think I 's tight,
Me not home an' comin' on night.
What 's dat stan'in' by de fence?
Pshaw! why don't I lu'n some sense?
    Git up, Suke — go long!

Guess I spent down dah at Jinks'
Mos' a dollah fur de drinks.
Bless yo'r soul, you see dat star?
Lawd, but won't Mirandy rar?
    Git up, Suke — go long!

Went dis mo'nin', hyeah it 's night,
Dah 's de cabin dah in sight.
Who 's dat stan'in' in de do'?
Dat must be Mirandy, sho',
    Git up, Suke — go long!

Got de close-stick in huh han',
Dat look funny, goodness lan',
Sakes alibe, but she look glum!
Hyeah, Mirandy, hyeah I come!
    Git up, Suke — go long!
Ef 't had n't a be'n fur you, you slow ole fool,
I 'd a' be'n home long fo' now!

Lyrics of Lowly Life.

DAWN.

AN angel, robed in spotless white,
    Bent down and kissed the sleeping
        Night.
Night woke to blush ; the sprite was gone.
Men saw the blush and called it Dawn.

A DROWSY DAY.

THE air is dark, the sky is gray,
    The misty shadows come and go,
And here within my dusky room
Each chair looks ghostly in the gloom.
    Outside the rain falls cold and slow —
Half-stinging drops, half-blinding spray.

Each slightest sound is magnified,
    For drowsy quiet holds her reign ;
The burnt stick in the fireplace breaks,
The nodding cat with start awakes,
    And then to sleep drops off again,
Unheeding Towser at her side.

Lyrics of Lowly Life.

I look far out across the lawn,
  Where huddled stand the silly sheep ;
My work lies idle at my hands,
My thoughts fly out like scattered strands
  Of thread, and on the verge of sleep —
Still half awake — I dream and yawn.

What spirits rise before my eyes !
  How various of kind and form !
Sweet memories of days long past,
The dreams of youth that could not last,
  Each smiling calm, each raging storm,
That swept across my early skies.

Half seen, the bare, gaunt-fingered boughs
  Before my window sweep and sway,
And chafe in tortures of unrest.
My chin sinks down upon my breast ;
  I cannot work on such a day,
But only sit and dream and drowse.

Lyrics of Lowly Life.

DIRGE.

PLACE this bunch of mignonette
 In her cold, dead hand;
When the golden sun is set,
 Where the poplars stand,
Bury her from sun and day,
Lay my little love away
  From my sight.

She was like a modest flower
 Blown in sunny June,
Warm as sun at noon's high hour,
 Chaster than the moon.
Ah, her day was brief and bright,
Earth has lost a star of light;
  She is dead.

Softly breathe her name to me, —
 Ah, I loved her so.
Gentle let your tribute be;
 None may better know
Her true worth than I who weep
O'er her as she lies asleep —
  Soft asleep.

Lyrics of Lowly Life.

Lay these lilies on her breast,
   They are not more white
Than the soul of her, at rest
   'Neath their petals bright.
Chant your aves soft and low,
Solemn be your tread and slow, —
     She is dead.

Lay her here beneath the grass,
   Cool and green and sweet,
Where the gentle brook may pass
   Crooning at her feet.
Nature's bards shall come and sing,
And the fairest flowers shall spring
     Where she lies.

Safe above the water's swirl,
   She has crossed the bar;
Earth has lost a precious pearl,
   Heaven has gained a star,
That shall ever sing and shine,
Till it quells this grief of mine
     For my love.

Lyrics of Lowly Life.

HYMN.

WHEN storms arise
And dark'ning skies
About me threat'ning lower,
To thee, O Lord, I raise mine eyes,
To thee my tortured spirit flies
For solace in that hour.

Thy mighty arm
Will let no harm
Come near me nor befall me;
Thy voice shall quiet my alarm,
When life's great battle waxeth warm —
No foeman shall appall me.

Upon thy breast
Secure I rest,
From sorrow and vexation;
No more by sinful cares oppressed,
But in thy presence ever blest,
O God of my salvation.

157

PREPARATION.

THE little bird sits in the nest and sings
　　A shy, soft song to the morning light;
And it flutters a little and prunes its wings.
　The song is halting and poor and brief,
　And the fluttering wings scarce stir a leaf;
But the note is a prelude to sweeter things,
　And the busy bill and the flutter slight
　Are proving the wings for a bolder flight!

THE DESERTED PLANTATION.

OH, de grubbin'-hoe 's a-rustin' in de co'nah,
　　An' de plow 's a-tumblin' down in de
　　　fiel',
While de whippo'will 's a-wailin' lak a mou'nah
　When his stubbo'n hea't is tryin' ha'd to
　　yiel'.

158

Lyrics of Lowly Life.

In de furrers whah de co'n was allus wavin',
   Now de weeds is growin' green an' rank an'
         tall;
An' de swallers roun' de whole place is a-bravin'
   Lak dey thought deir folks had allus owned it
         all.

An' de big house stan's all quiet lak an' solemn,
   Not a blessed soul in pa'lor, po'ch, er lawn;
Not a guest, ner not a ca'iage lef' to haul 'em,
   Fu' de ones dat tu'ned de latch-string out air
         gone.

An' de banjo's voice is silent in de qua'ters,
   D' ain't a hymn ner co'n-song ringin' in de
         air;
But de murmur of a branch's passin' waters
   Is de only soun' dat breks de stillness dere.

Whah 's de da'kies, dem dat used to be a-dancin'
   Evry night befo' de ole cabin do'?
Whah 's de chillun, dem dat used to be
         a-prancin'
   Er a-rollin' in de san' er on de flo'?

159

Lyrics of Lowly Life.

Whah 's ole Uncle Mordecai an' Uncle Aaron?
   Whah 's Aunt Doshy, Sam, an' Kit, an' all de
      res'?
Whah 's ole Tom de da'ky fiddlah, how 's he
      farin'?
   Whah 's de gals dat used to sing an' dance de
      bes'?

Gone ! not one o' dem is lef' to tell de story;
   Dey have lef' de deah ole place to fall away.
Could n't one o' dem dat seed it in its glory
   Stay to watch it in de hour of decay?

Dey have lef' de ole plantation to de swallers,
   But it hol's in me a lover till de las';
Fu' I fin' hyeah in de memory dat follers
   All dat loved me an' dat I loved in de pas'.

So I 'll stay an' watch de deah ole place an'
      tend it
   Ez I used to in de happy days gone by.
'Twell de othah Mastah thinks it 's time to end it,
   An' calls me to my qua'ters in de sky.

THE SECRET.

WHAT says the wind to the waving trees?
　　What says the wave to the river?
What means the sigh in the passing breeze?
　　Why do the rushes quiver?
Have you not heard the fainting cry
Of the flowers that said " Good-bye, good-bye " ?

List how the gray dove moans and grieves
　　Under the woodland cover;
List to the drift of the falling leaves,
　　List to the wail of the lover.
Have you not caught the message heard
Already by wave and breeze and bird?

Come, come away to the river's bank,
　　Come in the early morning;
Come when the grass with dew is dank,
　　There you will find the warning —
A hint in the kiss of the quickening air
Of the secret that birds and breezes bear.

Lyrics of Lowly Life.

THE WIND AND THE SEA.

I STOOD by the shore at the death of day,
   As the sun sank flaming red;
And the face of the waters that spread away
   Was as gray as the face of the dead.

And I heard the cry of the wanton sea
   And the moan of the wailing wind;
For love's sweet pain in his heart had he,
   But the gray old sea had sinned.

The wind was young and the sea was old,
   But their cries went up together;
The wind was warm and the sea was cold,
   For age makes wintry weather.

So they cried aloud and they wept amain,
   Till the sky grew dark to hear it;
And out of its folds crept the misty rain,
   In its shroud, like a troubled spirit.

Lyrics of Lowly Life.

For the wind was wild with a hopeless love,
   And the sea was sad at heart
At many a crime that he wot of,
   Wherein he had played his part.

He thought of the gallant ships gone down
   By the will of his wicked waves ;
And he thought how the churchyard in the town
   Held the sea-made widows' graves.

The wild wind thought of the love he had left
   Afar in an Eastern land,
And he longed, as long the much bereft,
   For the touch of her perfumed hand.

In his winding wail and his deep-heaved sigh
   His aching grief found vent ;
While the sea looked up at the bending sky
   And murmured : " I repent."

But e'en as he spoke, a ship came by,
   That bravely ploughed the main,
And a light came into the sea's green eye,
   And his heart grew hard again.

163

Then he spoke to the wind: " Friend, seest
    thou not
  Yon vessel is eastward bound?
Pray speed with it to the happy spot
  Where thy loved one may be found."

And the wind rose up in a dear delight,
  And after the good ship sped;
But the crafty sea by his wicked might
  Kept the vessel ever ahead.

Till the wind grew fierce in his despair,
  And white on the brow and lip.
He tore his garments and tore his hair,
  And fell on the flying ship.

And the ship went down, for a rock was there,
  And the sailless sea loomed black;
While burdened again with dole and care,
  The wind came moaning back.

And still he moans from his bosom hot
  Where his raging grief lies pent,
And ever when the ships come not,
  The sea says: " I repent."

RIDING TO TOWN.

WHEN labor is light and the morning is
      fair,
I find it a pleasure beyond all compare
To hitch up my nag and go hurrying down
And take Katie May for a ride into town;
   For bumpety-bump goes the wagon,
     But tra-la-la-la our lay.
There 's joy in a song as we rattle along
   In the light of the glorious day.

A coach would be fine, but a spring wagon 's
      good;
My jeans are a match for Kate's gingham and
      hood;
The hills take us up and the vales take us down,
But what matters that? we are riding to town,

Lyrics of Lowly Life.

And bumpety-bump goes the wagon,
    But tra-la-la-la sing we.
There's never a care may live in the air
    That is filled with the breath of our glee.

And after we've started, there's naught can
      repress
The thrill of our hearts in their wild happiness;
The heavens may smile or the heavens may frown,
And it's all one to us when we're riding to town.
    For bumpety-bump goes the wagon,
      But tra-la-la-la we shout,
For our hearts they are clear and there's noth-
      ing to fear,
    And we've never a pain nor a doubt.

The wagon is weak and the roadway is rough,
And tho' it is long it is not long enough,
For mid all my ecstasies this is the crown
To sit beside Katie and ride into town,
    When bumpety-bump goes the wagon,
      But tra-la-la-la our song;
And if I had my way, I'd be willing to pay
    If the road could be made twice as long.

Lyrics of Lowly Life.

WE WEAR THE MASK.

WE wear the mask that grins and lies,
　　It hides our cheeks and shades our
　　　　eyes, —
This debt we pay to human guile ;
With torn and bleeding hearts we smile,
And mouth with myriad subtleties.

Why should the world be over-wise,
In counting all our tears and sighs?
Nay, let them only see us, while
　　We wear the mask.

We smile, but, O great Christ, our cries
To thee from tortured souls arise.
We sing, but oh the clay is vile
Beneath our feet, and long the mile ;
But let the world dream otherwise,
　　We wear the mask !

THE MEADOW LARK.

THOUGH the winds be dank,
  And the sky be sober,
    And the grieving Day
    In a mantle gray
Hath let her waiting maiden robe her,—
  All the fields along
  I can hear the song
Of the meadow lark,
    As she flits and flutters,
    And laughs at the thunder when it mutters.
    O happy bird, of heart most gay
    To sing when skies are gray !

When the clouds are full,
  And the tempest master
    Lets the loud winds sweep
    From his bosom deep

Lyrics of Lowly Life.

Like heralds of some dire disaster,
　　Then the heart alone
　　To itself makes moan ;
And the songs come slow,
　　While the tears fall fleeter,
　　And silence than song by far seems
　　　sweeter.
　　Oh, few are they along the way
　　Who sing when skies are gray !

ONE LIFE.

OH, I am hurt to death, my Love ;
　　The shafts of Fate have pierced my
　　　striving heart,
And I am sick and weary of
　The endless pain and smart.
My soul is weary of the strife,
And chafes at life, and chafes at life.

169

Lyrics of Lowly Life.

Time mocks me with fair promises;
  A blooming future grows a barren past,
Like rain my fair full-blossomed trees
  Unburden in the blast.
The harvest fails on grain and tree,
Nor comes to me, nor comes to me.

The stream that bears my hopes abreast
  Turns ever from my way its pregnant tide.
My laden boat, torn from its rest,
  Drifts to the other side.
So all my hopes are set astray,
And drift away, and drift away.

The lark sings to me at the morn,
  And near me wings her skyward-soaring
     flight;
But pleasure dies as soon as born,
  The owl takes up the night,
And night seems long and doubly dark;
I miss the lark, I miss the lark.

Lyrics of Lowly Life.

Let others labor as they may,
 I'll sing and sigh alone, and write my line.
Their fate is theirs, or grave or gay,
 And mine shall still be mine.
I know the world holds joy and glee,
But not for me, — 't is not for me.

CHANGING TIME.

THE cloud looked in at the window,
 And said to the day, " Be dark ! "
And the roguish rain tapped hard on the pane,
 To stifle the song of the lark.

The wind sprang up in the tree tops
 And shrieked with a voice of death,
But the rough-voiced breeze, that shook the
   trees,
 Was touched with a violet's breath.

DEAD.

A KNOCK is at her door, but she is weak;
 Strange dews have washed the paint
  streaks from her cheek;
She does not rise, but, ah, this friend is known,
And knows that he will find her all alone.
So opens he the door, and with soft tread
Goes straightway to the richly curtained bed.
His soft hand on her dewy head he lays.
A strange white light she gives him for his gaze.
Then, looking on the glory of her charms,
He crushes her resistless in his arms.

Stand back! look not upon this bold embrace,
Nor view the calmness of the wanton's face;
With joy unspeakable and 'bated breath,
She keeps her last, long liaison with death!

A CONFIDENCE.

UNCLE JOHN, he makes me tired;
　　Thinks 'at he 's jest so all-fired
Smart, 'at he kin pick up, so,
Ever'thing he wants to know.
Tried to ketch me up last night,
But you bet I would n't bite.
I jest kep' the smoothes' face,
But I led him sich a chase,
Could n't corner me, you bet —
I skipped all the traps he set.
Makin' out he wan'ed to know
Who was this an' that girl's beau;
So 's he 'd find out, don't you see,
Who was goin' 'long with me.
But I answers jest ez sly,
An' I never winks my eye,
Tell he hollers with a whirl,

173

Lyrics of Lowly Life.

"Look here, ain't you got a girl?"
Y' ought 'o seen me spread my eyes,
Like he 'd took me by surprise,
An' I said, " Oh, Uncle John,
Never thought o' havin' one."
An' somehow that seemed to tickle
Him an' he shelled out a nickel.
Then you ought to seen me leave
Jest a-laffin' in my sleeve.
Fool him — well, I guess I did ;
He ain't on to this here kid.
Got a girl! well, I guess yes,
Got a dozen more or less,
But I got one reely one,
Not no foolin' ner no fun ;
Fur I 'm sweet on her, you see,
An' I ruther guess 'at she
Must be kinder sweet on me,
So we 're keepin' company.
Honest Injun! this is true,
Ever' word I 'm tellin' you !
But you won't be sich a scab
Ez to run aroun' an' blab.

Lyrics of Lowly Life.

Mebbe 't ain't the way with you,
But you know some fellers do.
Spoils a girl to let her know
'At you talk about her so.
Don't you know her? her name 's Liz,
Nicest girl in town she is.
Purty? ah, git out, you gilly —
Liz 'ud purt 'nigh knock you silly.
Y' ought 'o see her when she 's dressed
All up in her Sunday best,
All the fellers nudgin' me,
An' a-whisperin', gemunee!
Betcher life 'at I feel proud
When she passes by the crowd.
'T 's kinder nice to be a-goin'
With a girl 'at makes some showin' —
One you know 'at hain't no snide,
Makes you feel so satisfied.
An' I 'll tell you she 's a trump,
Never even seen her jump
Like some silly girls 'ud do,
When I 'd hide and holler " Boo! "
She 'd jest laff an' say " Git out!

Lyrics of Lowly Life.

What you hollerin' about?"
When some girls 'ud have a fit
That 'un don't git skeered a bit,
Never makes a bit o' row
When she sees a worm er cow.
Them kind 's few an' far between;
Bravest girl I ever seen.
Tell you 'nuther thing she 'll do,
Mebbe you won't think it 's true,
But if she 's jest got a dime
She 'll go halvers ever' time.
Ah, you goose, you need n't laff;
That 's the kinder girl to have.
If you knowed her like I do,
Guess you 'd kinder like her too.
Tell you somep'n' if you 'll swear
You won't tell it anywhere.
Oh, you got to cross yer heart
Earnest, truly, 'fore I start.
Well, one day I kissed her cheek;
Gee, but I felt cheap an' weak,
'Cause at first she kinder flared,
'N', gracious goodness! I was scared.

But I need n't been, fer la !
Why, she never told her ma.
That 's what I call grit, don't you?
Sich a girl 's worth stickin' to.

PHYLLIS.

PHYLLIS, ah, Phyllis, my life is a gray day,
  Few are my years, but my griefs are not
    few,
Ever to youth should each day be a May-day,
  Warm wind and rose-breath and diamonded
    dew —
Phyllis, ah, Phyllis, my life is a gray day.

Oh for the sunlight that shines on a May-day!
  Only the cloud hangeth over my life.
Love that should bring me youth's happiest
    heyday
  Brings me but seasons of sorrow and strife ;
Phyllis, ah, Phyllis, my life is a gray day.

Lyrics of Lowly Life.

Sunshine or shadow, or gold day or gray day,
  Life must be lived as our destinies rule;
Leisure or labor or work day or play day —
  Feasts for the famous and fun for the fool;
Phyllis, ah, Phyllis, my life is a gray day.

RIGHT'S SECURITY.

WHAT if the wind do howl without,
    And turn the creaking weather-vane;
What if the arrows of the rain
Do beat against the window-pane?
Art thou not armored strong and fast
Against the sallies of the blast?
Art thou not sheltered safe and well
Against the flood's insistent swell?

What boots it, that thou stand'st alone,
And laughest in the battle's face
When all the weak have fled the place
And let their feet and fears keep pace?

178

Lyrics of Lowly Life.

Thou wavest still thine ensign, high,
And shoutest thy loud battle-cry;
Higher than e'er the tempest roared,
It cleaves the silence like a sword.

Right arms and armors, too, that man
Who will not compromise with wrong;
Though single, he must front the throng,
And wage the battle hard and long.
Minorities, since time began,
Have shown the better side of man;
And often in the lists of Time
One man has made a cause sublime!

IF.

IF life were but a dream, my Love,
    And death the waking time;
If day had not a beam, my Love,
    And night had not a rhyme,—
            A barren, barren world were this
            Without one saving gleam;
            I'd only ask that with a kiss
            You'd wake me from the dream.

179

Lyrics of Lowly Life.

If dreaming were the sum of days,
  And loving were the bane ;
If battling for a wreath of bays
  Could soothe a heart in pain, —
        I 'd scorn the meed of battle's might,
        All other aims above
        I 'd choose the human's higher right,
        To suffer and to love !

THE SONG.

MY soul, lost in the music's mist,
    Roamed, rapt, 'neath skies of amethyst.
The cheerless streets grew summer meads,
The Son of Phœbus spurred his steeds,
And, wand'ring down the mazy tune,
December lost its way in June,
While from a verdant vale I heard
The piping of a love-lorn bird.

A something in the tender strain
Revived an old, long-conquered pain,

Lyrics of Lowly Life.

And as in depths of many seas,
My heart was drowned in memories.
The tears came welling to my eyes,
Nor could I ask it otherwise ;
For, oh ! a sweetness seems to last
Amid the dregs of sorrows past.

It stirred a chord that here of late
I 'd grown to think could not vibrate.
It brought me back the trust of youth,
The world again was joy and truth.
And Avice, blooming like a bride,
Once more stood trusting at my side.
But still, with bosom desolate,
The 'lorn bird sang to find his mate.

Then there are trees, and lights and stars,
The silv'ry tinkle of guitars ;
And throbs again as throbbed that waltz,
Before I knew that hearts were false.
Then like a cold wave on a shore,
Comes silence and she sings no more.
I wake, I breathe, I think again,
And walk the sordid ways of men.

SIGNS OF THE TIMES.

AIR a-gittin' cool an' coolah,
    Frost a-comin' in de night,
Hicka' nuts an' wa'nuts fallin',
    Possum keepin' out o' sight.
Tu'key struttin' in de ba'nya'd,
    Nary step so proud ez his;
Keep on struttin', Mistah Tu'key,
    Yo' do' know whut time it is.

Cidah press commence a-squeakin'
    Eatin' apples sto'ed away,
Chillun swa'min' 'roun' lak ho'nets,
    Huntin' aigs ermung de hay.
Mistah Tu'key keep on gobblin'
    At de geese a-flyin' souf,
Oomph! dat bird do' know whut 's comin';
    Ef he did he 'd shet his mouf.

Pumpkin gittin' good an' yallah
    Mek me open up my eyes;

182

Lyrics of Lowly Life.

Seems lak it 's a-lookin' at me
 Jes' a-la'in' dah sayin' " Pies."
Tu'key gobbler gwine 'roun' blowin',
 Gwine 'roun' gibbin' sass an' slack ;
Keep on talkin', Mistah Tu'key,
 You ain't seed no almanac.

Fa'mer walkin' th'oo de ba'nya'd
 Seein' how things is comin' on,
Sees ef all de fowls is fatt'nin' —
 Good times comin' sho 's you bo'n.
Hyeahs dat tu'key gobbler braggin',
 Den his face break in a smile —
Nebbah min', you sassy rascal,
 He 's gwine nab you atter while.

Choppin' suet in de kitchen,
 Stonin' raisins in de hall,
Beef a-cookin' fu' de mince meat,
 Spices groun' — I smell 'em all.
Look hyeah, Tu'key, stop dat gobblin',
 You ain' luned de sense ob feah,
You ol' fool, yo' naik 's in dangah,
 Do' you know Thanksgibbin 's hyeah?

183

WHY FADES A DREAM?

WHY fades a dream?
        An iridescent ray
Flecked in between the tryst
    Of night and day.
    Why fades a dream? —
Of consciousness the shade
Wrought out by lack of light and made
    Upon life's stream.
    Why fades a dream?

That thought may thrive,
    So fades the fleshless dream ;
Lest men should learn to trust
    The things that seem.
    So fades a dream,
That living thought may grow
And like a waxing star-beam glow
    Upon life's stream —
    So fades a dream.

Lyrics of Lowly Life.

THE SPARROW.

A LITTLE bird, with plumage brown,
    Beside my window flutters down,
A moment chirps its little strain,
Then taps upon my window-pane,
And chirps again, and hops along,
To call my notice to its song;
But I work on, nor heed its lay,
Till, in neglect, it flies away.

So birds of peace and hope and love
Come fluttering earthward from above,
To settle on life's window-sills,
And ease our load of earthly ills;
But we, in traffic's rush and din
Too deep engaged to let them in,
With deadened heart and sense plod on,
Nor know our loss till they are gone.

SPEAKIN' O' CHRISTMAS.

BREEZES blowin' middlin' brisk,
  Snow-flakes thro' the air a-whisk,
Fallin' kind o' soft an' light,
Not enough to make things white,
But jest sorter siftin' down
So 's to cover up the brown
Of the dark world's rugged ways
'N' make things look like holidays.
Not smoothed over, but jest specked,
Sorter strainin' fur effect,
An' not quite a-gittin' through
What it started in to do.
Mercy sakes ! it does seem queer
Christmas day is 'most nigh here.
Somehow it don't seem to me
Christmas like it used to be, —
Christmas with its ice an' snow,
Christmas of the long ago.
You could feel its stir an' hum

Lyrics of Lowly Life.

Weeks an' weeks before it come ;
Somethin' in the atmosphere
Told you when the day was near,
Did n't need no almanacs ;
That was one o' Nature's fac's.
Every cottage decked out gay —
Cedar wreaths an' holly spray —
An' the stores, how they were drest,
Tinsel tell you could n't rest ;
Every winder fixed up pat,
Candy canes, an' things like that ;
Noah's arks, an' guns, an' dolls,
An' all kinds o' fol-de-rols.
Then with frosty bells a-chime,
Slidin' down the hills o' time,
Right amidst the fun an' din
Christmas come a-bustlin' in,
Raised his cheery voice to call
Out a welcome to us all.
Hale and hearty, strong an' bluff,
That was Christmas, sure enough.
Snow knee-deep an' coastin' fine,
Frozen mill-ponds all ashine,

Lyrics of Lowly Life.

Seemin' jest to lay in wait,
Beggin' you to come an' skate.
An' you 'd git your gal an' go
Stumpin' cheerily thro' the snow,
Feelin' pleased an' skeert an' warm
'Cause she had a-holt yore arm.
Why, when Christmas come in, we
Spent the whole glad day in glee,
Havin' fun an' feastin' high
An' some courtin' on the sly.
Bustin' in some neighbor's door
An' then suddenly, before
He could give his voice a lift,
Yellin' at him, " Christmas gift."
Now sich things are never heard,
" Merry Christmas " is the word.
But it 's only change o' name,
An' means givin' jest the same.
There 's too many new-styled ways
Now about the holidays.
I 'd jest like once more to see
Christmas like it used to be !

Lyrics of Lowly Life.

LONESOME.

MOTHER's gone a-visitin' to spend a
    month er two,
An', oh, the house is lonesome ez a nest whose
    birds has flew
To other trees to build ag'in; the rooms seem
    jest so bare
That the echoes run like sperrits from the
    kitchen to the stair.
The shetters flap more lazy-like 'n what they
    used to do,
Sence mother's gone a-visitin' to spend a
    month er two.

We 've killed the fattest chicken an' we 've
    cooked her to a turn;
We 've made the richest gravy, but I jest don't
    give a durn
Fur nothin' 'at I drink er eat, er nothin' 'at I
    see.

Lyrics of Lowly Life.

The food ain't got the pleasant taste it used to
    have to me.
They's somep'n' stickin' in my throat ez tight
    ez hardened glue,
Sence mother's gone a-visitin' to spend a
    month er two.

The hollyhocks air jest ez pink, they're double
    ones at that,
An' I wuz prouder of 'em than a baby of a cat.
But now I don't go near 'em, though they nod
    an' blush at me,
Fur they's somep'n' seems to gall me in their
    keerless sort o' glee
An' all their fren'ly noddin' an' their blushin'
    seems to say :
"You're purty lonesome, John, old boy, sence
    mother's gone away."

The neighbors ain't so fren'ly ez it seems
    they'd ort to be ;
They seem to be a-lookin' kinder sideways like
    at me,

Lyrics of Lowly Life.

A-kinder feared they 'd tech me off ez ef I wuz
    a match,
An' all because 'at mother 's gone an' I 'm
    a-keepin' batch !
I 'm shore I don't do nothin' worse 'n what I
    used to do
'Fore mother went a-visitin' to spend a month
    er two.

The sparrers ac's more fearsome like an' won't
    hop quite so near,
The cricket's chirp is sadder, an' the sky ain't
    ha'f so clear ;
When ev'nin' comes, I set an' smoke tell my
    eyes begin to swim,
An' things aroun' commence to look all blurred
    an' faint an' dim.
Well, I guess I 'll have to own up 'at I 'm feelin'
    purty blue
Sence mother 's gone a-visitin' to spend a
    month er two.

Lyrics of Lowly Life.

GROWIN' GRAY.

HELLO, ole man, you 're a-gittin' gray,
  An' it beats ole Ned to see the way
'At the crow's feet 's a-getherin' aroun' yore eyes ;
Tho' it ought n't to cause me no su'prise,
Fur there 's many a sun 'at you 've seen rise
An' many a one you 've seen go down
Sence yore step was light an' yore hair was
    brown,
An' storms an' snows have had their way —
Hello, ole man, you 're a-gittin' gray.

Hello, ole man, you 're a-gittin' gray,
An' the youthful pranks 'at you used to play
Are dreams of a far past long ago
That lie in a heart where the fires burn low —
That has lost the flame though it kept the glow,
An' spite of drivin' snow an' storm,
Beats bravely on forever warm.
December holds the place of May —
Hello, ole man, you 're a-gittin' gray.

192

Lyrics of Lowly Life.

Hello, ole man, you 're a-gittin' gray —
Who cares what the carpin' youngsters say?
For, after all, when the tale is told,
Love proves if a man is young or old !
Old age can't make the heart grow cold
When it does the will of an honest mind ;
When it beats with love fur all mankind ;
Then the night but leads to a fairer day —
Hello, ole man, you 're a-gittin' gray !

TO THE MEMORY OF MARY YOUNG.

GOD has his plans, and what if we
   With our sight be too blind to see
Their full fruition ; cannot he,
Who made it, solve the mystery?
One whom we loved has fall'n asleep,
Not died ; although her calm be deep,
Some new, unknown, and strange surprise
In Heaven holds enrapt her eyes.

193

Lyrics of Lowly Life.

And can you blame her that her gaze
Is turned away from earthly ways,
When to her eyes God's light and love
Have giv'n the view of things above?
A gentle spirit sweetly good,
The pearl of precious womanhood ;
Who heard the voice of duty clear,
And found her mission soon and near.

She loved all nature, flowers fair,
The warmth of sun, the kiss of air,
The birds that filled the sky with song,
The stream that laughed its way along.
Her home to her was shrine and throne,
But one love held her not alone ;
She sought out poverty and grief,
Who touched her robe and found relief.

So sped she in her Master's work,
Too busy and too brave to shirk,
When through the silence, dusk and dim,
God called her and she fled to him.

Lyrics of Lowly Life.

We wonder at the early call,
And tears of sorrow can but fall
For her o'er whom we spread the pall;
But faith, sweet faith, is over all.

The house is dust, the voice is dumb,
But through undying years to come,
The spark that glowed within her soul
Shall light our footsteps to the goal.
She went her way; but oh, she trod
The path that led her straight to God.
Such lives as this put death to scorn;
They lose our day to find God's morn.

WHEN MALINDY SINGS.

G'WAY an' quit dat noise, Miss Lucy —
    Put dat music book away;
What 's de use to keep on tryin'?
    Ef you practise twell you 're gray,

Lyrics of Lowly Life.

You cain't sta't no notes a-flyin'
  Lak de ones dat rants and rings
F'om de kitchen to de big woods
  When Malindy sings.

You ain't got de nachel o'gans
  Fu' to make de soun' come right,
You ain't got de tu'ns an' twistin's
  Fu' to make it sweet an' light.
Tell you one thing now, Miss Lucy,
  An' I 'm tellin' you fu' true,
When hit comes to raal right singin',
  'T ain't no easy thing to do.

Easy 'nough fu' folks to hollah,
  Lookin' at de lines an' dots,
When dey ain't no one kin sence it,
  An' de chune comes in, in spots;
But fu' real melojous music,
  Dat jes' strikes yo' hea't and clings,
Jes' you stan' an' listen wif me
  When Malindy sings.

Lyrics of Lowly Life.

Ain't you nevah hyeahd Malindy?
  Blessed soul, tek up de cross !
Look hyeah, ain't you jokin', honey?
  Well, you don't know whut you los'.
Y' ought to hyeah dat gal a-wa'blin',
  Robins, la'ks, an' all dem things,
Heish dey moufs an' hides dey faces
  When Malindy sings.

Fiddlin' man jes' stop his fiddlin',
  Lay his fiddle on de she'f;
Mockin'-bird quit tryin' to whistle,
  'Cause he jes' so shamed hisse'f.
Folks a-playin' on de banjo
  Draps dey fingahs on de strings —
Bless yo' soul — fu'gits to move 'em,
  When Malindy sings.

She jes' spreads huh mouf and hollahs,
  " Come to Jesus," twell you hyeah
Sinnahs' tremblin' steps and voices,
  Timid-lak a-drawin' neah ;

Lyrics of Lowly Life.

Den she tu'ns to " Rock of Ages,"
  Simply to de cross she clings,
An' you fin' yo' teahs a-drappin'
  When Malindy sings.

Who dat says dat humble praises
  Wif de Master nevah counts?
Heish yo' mouf, I hyeah dat music,
  Ez hit rises up an' mounts —
Floatin' by de hills an' valleys,
  Way above dis buryin' sod,
Ez hit makes its way in glory
  To de very gates of God !

Oh, hit 's sweetah dan de music
  Of an edicated band ;
An' hit 's dearah dan de battle's
  Song o' triumph in de lan'.
It seems holier dan evenin'
  When de solemn chu'ch bell rings,
Ez I sit an' ca'mly listen
  While Malindy sings.

Lyrics of Lowly Life.

Towsah, stop dat ba'kin', hyeah me !
   Mandy, mek dat chile keep still ;
Don't you hyeah de echoes callin'
   F'om de valley to de hill?
Let me listen, I can hyeah it,
   Th'oo de bresh of angel's wings,
Sof' an' sweet, " Swing Low, Sweet Chariot,"
   Ez Malindy sings.

THE PARTY.

DEY had a gread big pahty down to Tom's
   de othah night ;
Was I dah? You bet! I nevah in my life see
   sich a sight ;
All de folks f'om fou' plantations was invited, an'
   dey come,
Dey come troopin' thick ez chillun when dey
   hyeahs a fife an' drum.
Evahbody dressed deir fines' — Heish yo' mouf
   an' git away,

Lyrics of Lowly Life.

Ain't seen no sich fancy dressin' sence las'
    quah'tly meetin' day;
Gals all dressed in silks an' satins, not a wrinkle
    ner a crease,
Eyes a-battin', teeth a-shinin', haih breshed back
    ez slick ez grease;
Sku'ts all tucked an' puffed an' ruffled, evah
    blessed seam an' stitch;
Ef you'd seen 'em wif deir mistus, could n't
    swahed to which was which.
Men all dressed up in Prince Alberts, swaller-
    tails 'u'd tek yo' bref!
I cain't tell you nothin' 'bout it, y' ought to seen
    it fu' yo'se'f.
Who was dah? Now who you askin'? How
    you 'spect I gwine to know?
You mus' think I stood an' counted evahbody at
    de do'.
Ole man Babah's house-boy Isaac, brung dat
    gal, Malindy Jane,
Huh a-hangin' to his elbow, him a-struttin' wif
    a cane;

Lyrics of Lowly Life.

My, but Hahvey Jones was jealous! seemed to
    stick him lak a tho'n;

But he laughed with Viney Cahteh, tryin' ha'd
    to not let on,

But a pusson would 'a' noticed f'om de d'rection
    of his look,

Dat he was watchin' ev'ry step dat Ike an'
    Lindy took.

Ike he foun' a cheer an' asked huh: "Won't
    you set down?" wif a smile,

An' she answe'd up a-bowin', "Oh, I reckon
    't ain't wuth while."

Dat was jes' fu' style, I reckon, 'cause she sot
    down jes' de same,

An' she stayed dah 'twell he fetched huh fu' to
    jine some so't o' game;

Den I hyeahd huh sayin' propah, ez she riz to
    go away,

"Oh, you raly mus' excuse me, fu' I hardly
    keers to play."

But I seen huh in a minute wif de othahs on de
    flo',

Lyrics of Lowly Life.

An' dah was n't any one o' dem a-playin' any
    mo' ;
Comin' down de flo' a-bowin' an' a-swayin' an'
    a-swingin',
Puttin' on huh high-toned mannahs all de time
    dat she was singin' :
" Oh, swing Johnny up an' down, swing him all
    aroun',
Swing Johnny up an' down, swing him all aroun',
Oh, swing Johnny up an' down, swing him all
    aroun',
Fa' you well, my dahlin'."
Had to laff at ole man Johnson, he 's a caution
    now, you bet —
Hittin' clost onto a hunderd, but he 's spry an'
    nimble yet ;
He 'lowed how a-so't o' gigglin', " I ain't ole,
    I 'll let you see,
D'ain't no use in gittin' feeble, now you young-
    stahs jes' watch me,"
An' he grabbed ole Aunt Marier — weighs th'ee
    hunderd mo' er less,

An' he spun huh 'roun' de cabin swingin' Johnny
lak de res'.

Evahbody laffed an' hollahed : " Go it ! Swing
huh, Uncle Jim !"

An' he swung huh too, I reckon, lak a youngstah,
who but him.

Dat was bettah 'n young Scott Thomas, tryin' to
be so awful smaht.

You know when dey gits to singin' an' dey
comes to dat ere paht :

"In some lady's new brick house,
In some lady's gyahden.

Ef you don't let me out, I will jump out,
So fa' you well, my dahlin'."

Den dey 's got a circle 'roun' you, an' you 's got
to break de line ;

Well, dat dahky was so anxious, lak to bust hisse'f a-tryin' ;

Kep' on blund'rin' 'roun' an' foolin' 'twell he
giv' one gread big jump,

Broke de line, an' lit head-fo'most in de fiah-
place right plump ;

203

Hit 'ad fiah in it, mind you ; well, I thought my
    soul I 'd bust,
Tried my best to keep f'om laffin', but hit
    seemed like die I must !
Y' ought to seen dat man a-scramblin' f'om de
    ashes an' de grime.
Did it bu'n him ! Sich a question, why he did n't
    give it time ;
Th'ow'd dem ashes and dem cindahs evah
    which-a-way I guess,
An' you nevah did, I reckon, clap yo' eyes on
    sich a mess ;
Fu' he sholy made a picter an' a funny one to
    boot,
Wif his clothes all full o' ashes an' his face all
    full o' soot.
Well, hit laked to stopped de pahty, an' I reckon
    lak ez not
Dat it would ef Tom's wife, Mandy, had n't
    happened on de spot,
To invite us out to suppah — well, we scrambled
    to de table,

An' I 'd lak to tell you 'bout it — what we had
 — but I ain't able,
Mention jes' a few things, dough I know I
 had n't orter,
Fu' I know 't will staht a hank'rin' an' yo' mouf
 'll 'mence to worter.
We had wheat bread white ez cotton an' a egg
 pone jes like gol',
Hog jole, bilin' hot an' steamin' roasted shoat
 an' ham sliced cold —
Look out ! What 's de mattah wif you ? Don't
 be fallin' on de flo' ;
Ef it 's go'n' to 'fect you dat way, I won't tell you
 nothin' mo'.
Dah now — well, we had hot chittlin's — now
 you 's tryin' ag'in to fall,
Cain't you stan' to hyeah about it ? S'pose you 'd
 been an' seed it all ;
Seed dem gread big sweet pertaters, layin' by
 de possum's side,
Seed dat coon in all his gravy, reckon den you 'd
 up and died !

Mandy 'lowed " you all mus' 'scuse me, d' wa'n't
much upon my she'ves,

But I's done my bes' to suit you, so set down
an' he'p yo'se'ves."

Tom, he 'lowed : " I don't b'lieve in 'pologisin'
an' perfessin',

Let 'em tek it lak dey ketch it. Eldah Thompson,
ask de blessin'."

Wish you'd seed dat colo'ed preachah cleah
his th'oat an' bow his head ;

One eye shet, an' one eye open, — dis is evah
wud he said :

" Lawd, look down in tendah mussy on sich gen-
erous hea'ts ez dese ;

Make us truly thankful, amen. Pass dat possum,
ef you please ! "

Well, we eat and drunk ouah po'tion, 'twell dah
was n't nothin' lef,

An' we felt jes' like new sausage, we was mos'
nigh stuffed to def !

Tom, he knowed how we'd be feelin', so he had
de fiddlah 'roun',

An' he made us cleah de cabin fu' to dance dat
 suppah down.

Jim, de fiddlah, chuned his fiddle, put some
 rosum on his bow,

Set a pine box on de table, mounted it an' let
 huh go !

He 's a fiddlah, now I tell you, an' he made dat
 fiddle ring,

'Twell de ol'est an' de lamest had to give deir
 feet a fling.

Jigs, cotillions, reels an' break-downs, cordrills
 an' a waltz er two ;

Bless yo' soul, dat music winged 'em an' dem
 people lak to flew.

Cripple Joe, de ole rheumatic, danced dat flo'
 f'om side to middle,

Th'owed away his crutch an' hopped it, what 's
 rheumatics 'ginst a fiddle ?

Eldah Thompson got so tickled dat he lak to
 los' his grace,

Had to tek bofe feet an' hol' dem so 's to keep
 'em in deir place.

An' de Christuns an' de sinnahs got so mixed
    up on dat flo',
Dat I don't see how dey 'd pahted ef de trump
    had chanced to blow.
Well, we danced dat way an' capahed in de mos'
    redic'lous way,
'Twell de roostahs in de bahnyard cleahed deir
    th'oats an' crowed fu' day.
Y' ought to been dah, fu' I tell you evahthing
    was rich an' prime,
An' dey ain't no use in talkin', we jes had one
    scrumptious time !